AF568080

FLAVOURS *of* INDIA

FLAVOURS *of* India

Heirloom Recipes from India's Kitchens

edited by
NEELA KAUSHIK AND SHIBANI SETHI

ALEPH

ALEPH BOOK COMPANY
An independent publishing firm
promoted by ***Rupa Publications India***

First published in India in 2025 by
Aleph Book Company
7/16 Ansari Road, Daryaganj
New Delhi 110 002

ISBN: 978-93-6523-338-4

1 3 5 7 9 10 8 6 4 2

Printed and bound in India

Contents

Curries

Chicken

Mutton

Seafood

Pickles and Chutneys

Sweets

Beverages

Panagam

by Neela Kaushik, Tamil Nadu

Panagam, a traditional drink offered to the Gods every day, has been an integral part of our family rituals for as long as I can remember. Growing up, the ringing of the puja bell by my father signalled the end of evening prayers. My sister and I would race to the puja room, recite our prayers hastily, and then eagerly extend our cupped palms to receive the Panagam. Carefully, my father would pour the sacred drink into our palms, ensuring not a drop spilled. We would savour its cool and refreshing taste—a delightful blend of sweet and tangy flavours.

My grandfather often reminded us of Panagam's benefits, emphasizing that it was an effective coolant, perfect for the hot, humid summers of the South. I vividly recall my amma preparing Panagam every day, my father offering it to the Gods, and then lovingly sharing it with us. These memories fill my heart with joy and nostalgia.

Even now, whenever I prepare or taste this drink, I am transported to those warm evenings, filled with love, devotion, and the simple joys of childhood. To me, Panagam is more than just a drink—it's a cherished memory and a comforting reminder of family and tradition.

PANAGAM
(Spiced Jaggery Drink)

NEELA KAUSHIK

TAMIL NADU

SERVES: 2

PREPARATION TIME: 5 MINUTES

COOK TIME: 5 MINUTES

INGREDIENTS

Water	240 ml
Jaggery	60 gms, powdered
Dry ginger powder	½ tsp
Cardamom	4 pods, pounded coarsely
Pepper powder	½ tsp
Lemon juice	½ tsp
Edible camphor	¼ tsp, powdered
Salt	to taste
Basil	10–12 leaves

METHOD

Heat 240 ml of water in a saucepan and bring it to a boil.

Once the water begins boiling, add dry ginger powder, cardamom powder, and pepper powder. Let the mixture simmer briefly, and then turn off the heat.

Add the powdered jaggery to the hot mixture and stir until it fully dissolves. Allow the mixture to cool completely.

Once cooled, strain the mixture through a fine sieve. To the strained mixture, add lemon juice and edible camphor and mix well. Adjust the taste by adding a pinch of salt.

Finally, tear some basil leaves roughly by hand and mix them into the beverage.

Your Panagam is now ready to serve.

Note: Panagam can be served immediately at room temperature or can be chilled and served later.

Bael ka Sherbet

by Ambika Rikhye, New Delhi

I come from a simple middle-class family where we enjoyed the little pleasures in life. My mother was a teacher at the same school my brother and I attended. On those scorching summer days, just as we dragged ourselves home, exhausted and sticky, Mummy would whip up a glass of her famous Bael ka Sherbet for us. She was a master of this magical golden nectar, preparing the concentrate ahead of time and chilling it in the fridge. My brother and I would sit in front of the cooler, clutching our frosty glasses and relishing every sip.

Now, unlike my mother, my cooking usually falls into one of two categories: 'edible' and 'maybe next time'. But when it comes to a few dishes—and Bael ka Sherbet is definitely one of them—I manage to surprise even myself. Found in abundance in North India during the summer, this humble fruit is a true hero for the tummy with its cooling and healing properties. But let's be honest, it's an acquired taste. In fact, someone once took a sip of this exotic sherbet and compared it to melted rubber. Now, I have no idea how they know what melted rubber tastes like!

But here's the thing: the moment I catch a whiff of bael, I'm transported to those innocent, carefree childhood days—back to the golden years when time moved slower, the company was warmer, and simple, homemade food tasted like heaven. It's funny how a fruit can hold so much nostalgia, even if it's not everyone's cup of...well, sherbet.

BAEL KA SHERBET
(Wood Apple Cooler)

AMBIKA RIKHYE NEW DELHI

SERVES: 4–5 PREPARATION TIME: 20 MINUTES

INGREDIENTS

Bael (wood apple)	1 fruit, large
Desi khaand (unrefined sugar)	2–3 tbsp
Water	120 ml (approx.)
Lemon juice (optional)	2 tsp

METHOD

Break open the bael and scoop the pulp into a bowl with a spoon.

Add water and desi khaand to the pulp and begin mashing with your hands. Continue mashing until the pulp starts to dissolve in the water, and the seeds and fibres separate.

Strain the mixture using a fine sieve to get a smooth pulp.

Adjust the sweetness by adding more khaand or a dash of lemon juice, according to your taste.

While serving, dilute the mixture with more water to get your preferred consistency.

Serving suggestion: For the best taste, serve chilled.

Note: For optimal flavour, it's recommended not to use jaggery or brown sugar in this recipe. If desi khaand is unavailable, powdered white sugar can be used instead.

Borhani

by Munmun Mukherjee, West Bengal

Borhani is a treasured part of my culinary heritage, rich with memories and cultural significance. During my university days, I savoured it at my best friend's home and at lively wedding celebrations. My friend's mother would prepare it with great care, blending yogurt with green chillies, mint, sugar, and salt to create a refreshing and vibrant drink.

Every glass of Borhani I had was a reflection of the joyful gatherings and strong bonds I formed during those times, making it a cherished part of my life.

Now, making Borhani allows me to reconnect with those warm memories and the spirit of hospitality. This heirloom recipe is more than just a drink—it represents family, tradition, and the comforting essence of home.

BORHANI
(Spiced Yogurt Drink)

MUNMUN MUKHERJEE — WEST BENGAL

SERVES: 3–4 — PREPARATION TIME: 25 MINUTES

INGREDIENTS

Yogurt	300 gms, thickened
Cumin powder	1 tsp, roasted

White pepper powder	½ tsp
Ginger paste	½ tsp
White mustard paste	1 tsp
Coriander leaf paste	1 tsp
Mint leaf paste	1 tsp
Green chilli paste	1 tsp
Black salt	A pinch
Sugar	30 gms
Salt	to taste
Water	80 ml
Coriander leaves	to garnish
Mint leaves	to garnish

METHOD

To thicken the yogurt, tie it in a muslin cloth and hang it for a while to allow the excess water to drain out.

In a mixing bowl, take the thickened yogurt and add roasted cumin powder, white pepper powder, black salt, and finely ground ginger paste, white mustard paste, coriander leaf paste, mint leaf paste, and green chilli paste.

Mix all the ingredients thoroughly.

Then, add 10 grams of sugar and salt to taste, adjusting both according to your preference.

Using a whisk or blender, mix everything until well combined. Then slowly add water, and stir until the mixture is smooth and colourful.

Put the drink in the refrigerator and let it rest for a few hours to blend the flavours and enhance its refreshing quality.

Serving suggestion: Before serving, garnish the Borhani with a few mint and coriander leaves to add a dash of colour and freshness. Serve it with grilled kebabs like Seekh Kebabs, Shami Kebabs, or Chicken Tikka. The cool, spicy drink offers a refreshing contrast to the smoky, savoury meat.

Note: Borhani is a classic accompaniment to rich, flavourful rice dishes like Dhakai Tehari, Biryani, or Pilaf. The tangy and spicy yogurt drink helps balance the richness and spices of these dishes. Borhani also serves as a palate cleanser, making it an essential part of festive meals.

Aam Panna

by Pooja Nagalia, Uttar Pradesh

My sister and I were born and raised in North India, where the summers were scorching, and the elders were always worried about keeping us hydrated—something we were too busy to care about. Our mom and grandmother were no different, and since soda or store-bought juices were completely off-limits during our childhood, we were constantly served all kinds of delicious, cooling homemade drinks.

My favourite among them was the sweet yet tangy Aam Panna. I eagerly looked forward to guzzling down that refreshing drink as soon as we got home from school! In fact, it became so special to me that it was the very first thing I learned to make when I finally ventured into the kitchen as a teen. My grandmother was more than happy to oblige, teaching us hands-on. It was a family project, with my sister diligently plucking mint leaves and me squeezing the pulp out of those boiled raw mangoes.

The aroma of boiled mangoes mixed with mint leaves, black salt, and cumin powder is forever imprinted in my memory, along with the laughter that accompanied any family project we took on. Now, I carry on this tradition by making the beloved Aam Panna for my two children every summer, and we lovingly continue this ritual.

AAM PANNA
(Raw Mango Cooler)

POOJA NAGALIA

UTTAR PRADESH

SERVES: 4–6

PREPARATION TIME: 10 MINUTES

COOK TIME: 30 MINUTES

INGREDIENTS

Raw mangoes	150 gms
Mint leaves	10 gms
Black salt	50 gms
Sugar	1 tsp
Salt	1 tsp
Cumin powder	1 tsp, roasted
Water	150 ml, to boil mangoes

METHOD

Wash the mangoes thoroughly and boil them in a pressure cooker with 150 ml of water until it releases 1 whistle.

Allow the boiled mangoes to cool, peel them, and squeeze out all the pulp. Discard the mango pits.

Then, transfer the pulp to a mixer along with the mint leaves and grind them well. Strain the mixture through a fine mesh sieve to get a smooth pulp.

In a pan, combine the smooth mango-mint pulp with sugar, water, black salt, regular salt, and roasted cumin powder.

Bring the mixture to a boil and let it simmer for 4–5 minutes.

Turn off the flame and let the mixture cool. Pour the cooled mixture into a clear glass bottle and store it in the refrigerator to extend its shelf life.

Serving suggestion: Take 2–3 tablespoonfuls of the drink in a glass, add chilled water, and top it with some ice cubes and a sprig of mint leaves to garnish.

Note: The sweetness can be adjusted as per personal preference.

Rajasthani Bajra Raab
by Surbhi Bhandari, Rajasthan

Raab is a cherished Marwari drink, steeped in tradition and versatility. The beauty of raab lies in its ability to adapt to the changing seasons—cold and refreshing in the summer, warm and comforting in the winter. I vividly remember my dadi making it almost every day during the colder months. In the evenings, we would gather around, eagerly waiting for a warm bowl of raab, our version of 'soup' in those simpler times.

In the summer, raab is made with whole wheat and barley flours, and left to ferment overnight. The next day, it's enjoyed chilled with chopped onions, dahi, and khakhra—a perfect way to beat the heat. But in the winter, the recipe changes. Dadi would use bajra flour, which brings warmth to the body, and serve it hot as a soup. The best part was the charcoal dhungaar, which added a distinct smoky flavour, making each sip deeply satisfying.

For us, raab wasn't just a drink; it was a symbol of Dadi's love, warmth, and the simple joys she brought into our home.

RAJASTHANI BAJRA RAAB
(Rajasthani Pearl Millet Comfort Soup)

SURBHI BHANDARI — RAJASTHAN

SERVES: 4 — PREPARATION TIME: 20 MINUTES

COOK TIME: 40–45 MINUTES

INGREDIENTS

Dahi (curd)	125 gms
Water	950 ml
Bajra flour (pearl millet flour)	30 gms
Ginger	1 tsp, grated
Cumin powder	½ tsp, roasted
Salt	to taste
Coriander leaves	to garnish
Charcoal	1 piece
Desi ghee	1 tsp

METHOD

In a pan, mix curd, water, bajra flour, salt, ginger, and cumin powder. Whisk thoroughly to ensure there are no lumps.

Place the pan on the stove and stir continuously for the first 5–7 minutes to prevent curdling. Continue cooking for 15–20 minutes until the mixture thickens. Turn off the stove.

Heat a piece of charcoal over an open flame until it is red-hot. Place a small metal bowl in the centre of the raab pan. Make sure that the bowl is elevated enough so that the raab does not spill into it.

Carefully, place the hot charcoal in the bowl. Pour 1 tsp ghee on the charcoal and immediately cover the pan with a lid to trap the smoke. Let it sit for 15 minutes until the smoke infuses into the raab.

Uncover the pan and remove the bowl with the charcoal piece.

Garnish with some chopped coriander and roasted cumin powder before serving.

Serving suggestion: Serve the raab hot for the best flavour and warmth.

Vegetarian Snacks

Badeel

by Ratna Pande, Uttarakhand

This recipe is a cherished family snack passed down through generations, from my grandmom to my mom and now to me. It's ideal for tiffins, party starters, or as a side dish. Because it boasts of a long shelf life even without refrigeration, I've often carried it in airtight steel boxes on my travels. Made from lentils, it's not only nutritious but also flavourful, thanks to the seasoning. Since my mom's passing, preparing this snack has become a way to honour her memory and revisit cherished moments—it surpasses any ready-made options available today.

The non-fried version is an excellent choice for those on a diet, while the fried version is perfect for active children involved in sports and school. The tempering enhances its taste and makes it easy to digest, despite being made from pulses. Its soft texture made it a favourite of my grandmom in her old age—it became her go-to snack as she found it comforting and relied on it for warmth. This versatile dish truly caters to all ages and occasions, making it a timeless family favourite.

BADEEL
(Spiced Lentil Bites)

RATNA PANDE | UTTARAKHAND

SERVES: 4–5 | PREPARATION TIME: 1 HOUR 45 MINUTES

COOK TIME: 30–40 MINUTES

INGREDIENTS

Chana dal (split Bengal gram)	200 gms
Green chillies	4
Garlic	4–5 cloves
Ginger	2-inch piece
Red chilli powder	1 tsp
Coriander powder	1 tsp
Turmeric powder	½ tsp
Onion	1 tbsp, chopped
Coriander leaves	25 gms, chopped
Oil	1 tbsp
Chilli flakes	1 tbsp, to garnish
Salt	to taste

FOR TEMPERING:

Mustard oil	2 tsp
Mustard seeds	¼ tsp
Curry leaves	8–10

METHOD

Soak chana dal in water for 60–90 minutes. Wet grind the soaked dal to a smooth paste and keep aside.

Grind green chillies, ginger, and garlic to form a paste and set aside.

Heat oil in a pan and fry chopped onion till golden brown. Add red chilli powder, turmeric powder, and coriander powder.

Mix well and let it cook for 2 minutes. Put in salt and the chilli-ginger-garlic paste. Cook again for 3–4 minutes.

Add the lentil paste to the pan. Stir continuously with a spatula and cook for 20–30 minutes until it thickens into a well-roasted paste.

Add chopped coriander leaves and mix well.

Spread the mixture evenly to ½-inch thickness on a greased thali or flat tray.

If it's too hot outside, refrigerate it for 1 hour. Otherwise, allow it to cool at room temperature.

Once set, insert a toothpick into the centre. If it comes out clean, Badeel is ready. Cut into rectangular pieces and arrange them on a plate nicely.

Now, heat 2 tsp of mustard oil, add ¼ tsp of mustard seeds, and 8–10 curry leaves. Let them splutter. Garnish the Badeel by pouring this tempering over the pieces.

Serving suggestion: Serve as is or pair with hemp chutney.

Note: The Badeel pieces can also be deep-fried before garnishing. They can be stored in an airtight container for up to a week.

Murauri
by Priya Baranwal, Bihar

Winter evenings were always a special time spent in the warm kitchen with Mom, sharing the stories of the day. But on the days Murauri was made, the experience became even more delightful as we got to eat them fresh and hot, right there in the kitchen. My two sisters and I would gather around Mom, not giving her a moment's rest until our tummies were full.

The real fun, however, began the next day when we'd all scramble for the leftovers. Murauri with tea tasted heavenly, and it often led to playful fights over who got the biggest share. Yet somehow, Mom always managed to give us each an equal share. Now that I'm a mom myself, I realize the secret behind her effortless fairness—she had been carefully counting and setting them aside for us, ensuring we each had our fair share the next morning too.

MURAURI
(Savoury Rice Flour and Radish Poori)

PRIYA BARANWAL | BIHAR

SERVES: 3–4 | PREPARATION TIME: 30 MINUTES

COOK TIME: 15 MINUTES

INGREDIENTS

Radish	500 gms, grated
Green chillies	3–4, chopped
Ginger	1 inch, grated
Salt	to taste
Carom seeds	1 tsp, crushed with hands
Black caraway seeds	1 tsp, crushed with hands
Coriander leaves	3–4 tbsp, chopped
Rice flour	300 gms
Oil	to fry
Lukewarm water	100 ml

METHOD

Heat a deep and thick-bottomed pan on medium heat. Add some oil, add the grated radish, and sauté for 30 seconds.

Add 100 ml of normal temperature/lukewarm water. Cover and cook for 5 minutes.

Add salt and continue cooking on low heat until the radish becomes soft.

Stir in the rest of the ingredients, except rice flour and oil. Mix well and cook for 2 minutes.

Gradually add rice flour, 2 tablespoons at a time.

Stir well and cook for 1 more minute until it takes a dough-like consistency.

Turn off the stove, cover the pan, and let it rest for 10 more minutes. Ensure the pan is covered properly.

Transfer the mixture to a wide plate or pan. Once it cools down slightly and is just warm enough to touch, knead it gently into a smooth dough. If it gets too cold, it won't hold together properly for shaping.

Apply oil on your palms and shape the dough into small balls, keeping the dough covered with a moist cotton cloth at all times to avoid drying out.

Now, the traditional way is to press the dough balls between your palms to form thick pooris. Alternatively, roll them using a rolling pin, and cut them into circles using a steel glass, bowl, or cookie cutter.

Heat enough oil in a wok for deep frying. Fry the pooris until golden and crispy; and your Murauri is ready.

Serving suggestion: Serve the Murauri with green coriander chutney and achaar (especially garlic or mango achaar).

Notes: Adjust the amount of rice flour as needed, depending on the water used. This is a traditional winter delicacy but can be enjoyed as soon as fresh radish starts appearing in the market. It's best to use the prepared dough immediately; however, fried Murauri can be stored and tastes even better the next day.

Dudhi na Muthiya
by Shailee Shah, Gujarat

Muthiya holds a special place in my heart, evoking sweet memories of childhood afternoons spent in the kitchen with my mom. True to its name, it's made with your mutthi (fist), and I still remember how my small fists back then shaped perfect little muthiyas! We would make them with all sorts of seasonal vegetables—a perfect teatime snack that paired so well with coriander chutney and a sprinkle of achaar masala.

The best part, though, was the chitchat that flowed as freely as the tea, making every bite taste even better. Even my non-Gujarati friends in school couldn't resist this treat, asking me to bring it at least once a week!

Muthiya is not just a snack for me—it's a taste of home, a bite of nostalgia, and a reminder of those cherished moments with my mom.

DUDHI NA MUTHIYA
(Steamed Bottle Gourd Dumplings)

SHAILEE SHAH — GUJARAT

SERVES: 2 — PREPARATION TIME: 12–15 MINUTES

COOK TIME: 25 MINUTES

INGREDIENTS

Dudhi (bottle gourd)	250 gms, grated
Carrot (optional)	1, medium-sized, grated
Coriander leaves	10 gms
Wheat flour	150 gms
Sooji (semolina)	50 gms
Besan (chickpea flour)	25 gms
Red chilli powder	½ tbsp or to taste
Turmeric powder	½ tsp
Coriander powder	1 tbsp
Green chilli paste	1 tbsp
Ginger paste	½ tsp
Oil	1 tbsp
Sesame seeds	1 tbsp
Sugar	1½ tbsp
Lemon juice	1 tbsp
Yogurt	1 tbsp
Salt	to taste
Coriander leaves	chopped, to garnish
Fresh coconut	grated, to garnish

FOR TEMPERING:

Oil	2 tbsp
Mustard seeds	1 tsp
Sesame seeds	1 tsp
Asafoetida	a pinch
Curry leaves	a sprig

METHOD

Combine all the ingredients (except for the ones for the tempering and garnish) in a bowl. Mix well with your hands and roll into a dough. There is no need to add water as dudhi will release enough water for the dough.

Keep it aside for 15 minutes. If the dough turns too loose, add more wheat flour to thicken it. If it feels too tight, sprinkle a little water and mix again. The dough should have a semi-thick consistency.

Now, grease a steel plate with oil and keep it in the steamer.

Then, grease your hands with a little oil. Take small portions of the dough and shape them into cylindrical rolls. Arrange the rolls on the greased steel plate inside the steamer.

Cover the steamer and steam the muthiyas for 15–20 minutes. Insert a knife into the rolls to check if the muthiyas are done. If it comes out clean, they are ready!

Remove them from the steamer and let them cool. Once cooled, cut the rolls into thick roundels, approximately 1 cm each.

For tempering, heat oil in a pan. Add mustard seeds and let them splutter. Add curry leaves and asafoetida, followed by sesame seeds. Then, add the sliced muthiyas as well.

Gently toss to coat the muthiyas with the tempering. Roast till they become a little crisp, ensuring they are evenly roasted on both sides.

Garnish with coriander leaves and grated coconut.

Serving suggestion: Serve with a cup of tea.

Doli Wali Roti

by Simmi Babbar, Multan

Marrying into a Multani family with a Peshawari background has been a delightful culinary journey. Peshawari cuisine is known for its luxurious flavours, while Multani cuisine tends to be much simpler, often featuring a distinctive khatta masala. This balance between indulgence and restraint has made exploring these traditions both exciting and enriching.

My mother-in-law, an exceptional cook, introduced me to famous Multani dishes like Rallimili Sabzi, Doli Wali Roti, Sohani Halwa, Angoori Halwa, and Mukund Wadi Aloo. She was my mentor in the kitchen, and one of the most cherished recipes I learned from her was Doli Wali Roti. Curious about the name, I once asked my mother-in-law why it's called Doli Wali Roti. She explained that in earlier times, when baraats had to travel long distances, these rotis were given to the groom's party during the vidai ceremony so they could have something to eat on the way. With a shelf life of four to five days, Doli Wali Roti was an ideal travel food, perfectly suited for long journeys.

This is a dish deeply rooted in tradition but sadly fading with time. Its lengthy cooking process makes it less appealing to the younger generation, and I often wonder if its legacy will endure.

DOLI WALI ROTI
(Stuffed Deep-fried Flatbread with Lentils)

SIMMI BABBAR — MULTAN

MAKES: 10–12 ROTIS — PREPARATION TIME: 35–36 HOURS

COOK TIME: 1 HOUR

INGREDIENTS

FOR THE YEAST:

Black cardamom	5–6 seeds
Fennel seeds	2 tbsp
Chana dal	2 tbsp
Poppy seeds	2 tbsp
Cloves	10
Sugar	3 tbsp
Water	300 ml
Flour	2 tsp

FOR THE DOUGH:

Sugar	2 tsp
Flour	400 gms
Salt	1 tsp
Lukewarm water	to knead
Oil	to fry

FOR THE STUFFING:

Chana dal	200 gms
Salt	to taste
Cumin seeds	½ tsp
Turmeric powder	¼ tsp
Red chilli powder	1 tsp
Coriander powder	1 tsp
Garam masala	½ tsp
Oil	2 tsp

METHOD

To prepare the yeast, take a pan, add water, poppy seeds, cardamom, fennel seeds, chana dal, cloves, and sugar. Boil the mixture for five minutes. Add 2 teaspoons of flour and stir well. Keep it in a warm place and let it rest for the next 24–30 hours.

Now, to make the dough, in a large bowl or paraat, mix flour, salt, sugar, and the prepared yeast mixture. Knead the mixture with lukewarm water to make a soft dough. Cover it with a cloth and keep it in a warm place for 5–6 hours.

For the stuffing, boil chana dal until it softens. Take a small pan and heat oil in it. Add cumin seeds, red chilli powder, turmeric powder, coriander powder, garam masala, and salt to the oil, and let them splutter. Add this tempering to the boiled chana dal.

After 5–6 hours, the dough will have doubled in volume. Divide the dough into small portions and shape them into balls (pedas). Flatten each ball slightly, stuff it with the prepared dal mixture, and seal the edges tightly. With soft hands, keep flattening the stuffed dough with your palms to form a disc, similar to a poori or kachori.

For the final step, take a heavy-bottomed pan and heat oil in it over a medium-low flame. Deep fry the prepared discs until they turn golden brown on both sides. Doli Wali Rotis are ready to be served!

Serving suggestion: Serve it hot with boondi raita.

Koraishutir Kochuri
by Manisha Mukherji, West Bengal

I'm a North Indian who married into a Bengali family, and today, I can proudly say I've mastered nearly all traditional Bengali recipes—both vegetarian and non-vegetarian. Among them, my absolute favourite is Koraishutir Kochuri, a luchi stuffed with a delicious, spiced mixture of cooked peas.

I learned to make this dish during the first year of my marriage from my husband's nani. She was an incredible, warm-hearted woman who welcomed me with open arms and showered me with love. She continues to hold a very special place in my heart. This deep connection makes Koraishutir Kochuri all the more meaningful to me. So, it's no surprise that this dish is my favourite Bengali recipe.

In fact, my husband's family often says that I make it better than most native Bengalis. Moments like these remind me of how this dish has become a symbol of love and belonging.

KORAISHUTIR KOCHURI
(Green Pea-stuffed Luchi)

MANISHA MUKHERJI | WEST BENGAL

SERVES: 4–6 | PREPARATION TIME: 15 MINUTES

COOK TIME: 50 MINUTES

INGREDIENTS

Peas	250 gms
Ginger	3–4 inch
Green chillies	2–3
Mustard oil	2 tbsp
Asafoetida	a pinch
Fennel seeds	2 tbsp
Cumin seeds	2 tbsp
Maida (all-purpose flour)	120 gms
Wheat flour	120 gms
Oil	2 tbsp, warm
Lukewarm water	to knead
Salt	to taste
Oil	to fry

METHOD

Dry roast the fennel seeds and cumin seeds until aromatic. Grind them into a fine powder and keep aside.

Now, grind the peas with ginger and green chillies into a thick, smooth paste. Add a little water if required.

In a pan, heat mustard oil and temper it with asafoetida. Add the pea mixture to the pan and cook on a low flame until it is fully cooked and dry.

Mix in about half of the dry-roasted spice powder and season with salt to taste. Set the filling aside to cool.

In a bowl, mix the flours, a teaspoon of the dry-roasted spice powder, a pinch of salt, and warm oil. Gradually, add lukewarm water and knead into a smooth, pliable dough. Cover it with a moist cloth and let it rest for 10–15 minutes.

Now, divide the dough into small balls and flatten them a little. Place a small portion of the pea filling in the centre. Carefully gather and seal all the ends, ensuring there are no tears. Roll the stuffed dough balls into thin pooris.

In a wok, heat oil for frying. To check the temperature, drop a small ball of dough into the oil, it should float up to the surface quickly.

Fry the pooris one at a time until light golden brown on both sides. Remove and drain on paper towels.

Serving suggestion: Serve them with Aloo Dum or Mutton Curry.

Meethe Roat

by Upreet Khanna, Punjab

Every monsoon and winter, the sweet, earthy scent of Meethe Roat fills our home. It is a comforting reminder of Biji, my grandmother. As the rain patters against the windowpanes and mist envelops the trees, the aroma of this cherished family heirloom wafts through the air. Biji taught me this recipe, a tradition passed down through generations. This flatbread is much more than a dish—it's a taste of history and a symbol of our culture.

I still remember the excitement of rainy days. Our house used to be filled with the intoxicating aroma of Meethe Roat made in June and savoured throughout the monsoon season. The entire household would gather on the veranda, sharing stories and laughter while enjoying the warm, spiced bread with steaming cups of chai. Some of us relished it while sitting on a manji (cot), while others simply sat on the floor. Each bite was a journey back in time, carrying an essence of tradition and a connection to the past. Monsoon evenings were filled with sweet memories of playing antakshari or carrom, and the elders who savoured the roat with fresh milk cream or white butter alongside a hot cup of chai.

Today, as I make Meethe Roat, these cherished moments come rushing back, giving a sense of peace and belonging. It is a recipe that binds us together as a family. With every bite,

I remember my biji's love and the countless memories we've shared.

MEETHE ROAT
(Sweet Wheat Flour Bread)

UPREET KHANNA PUNJAB

SERVES: 5–6

PREPARATION TIME: 25 MINUTES

COOK TIME: 25 MINUTES

INGREDIENTS

Water	100 ml
Cardamom powder	¼ tsp
Fennel seeds	2 gms
Baking soda	a pinch
Black peppercorns	¼ tsp, crushed
Poppy seeds (khus khus)	2 gms
Jaggery	200 gms
Wheat flour	500 gms
Desi ghee	2 tbsp and to cook the roat

METHOD

Heat water in a pan until it starts to boil. Transfer it to a mixing bowl.

Add cardamom powder, fennel seeds, black peppercorns, poppy seeds, and jaggery to the water.

Stir well until the jaggery dissolves completely.

Gradually incorporate the wheat flour into the mixture, mixing thoroughly to form a dough.

Add 2 tablespoons of ghee and a pinch of baking soda. Knead the dough until it is smooth and pliable. Cover the dough with a cloth and let it rest for 15 minutes.

Divide the dough into equal portions and roll each portion into small balls.

Lightly dust a rolling board with flour and roll each ball into a small, thick roti of about 6–7 mm thickness. For a uniform shape, use a circular steel cutter, if desired.

To cook the roti, heat desi ghee in a pan. Fry the rotis one at a time until golden brown on both sides. Use medium heat to ensure the inside cooks thoroughly.

After frying, place each roti on a sheet of butter paper or a clean cotton cloth. Allow them to cool completely. Store the cooled rotis in a clean steel or glass jar to maintain their freshness.

Serving suggestion: Serve Meethe Roat with a hot cup of tea or enjoy them with a dollop of butter or fresh milk cream, especially during the monsoon season.

Pesarattu Upma

by Supriya Deverkonda, Andhra Pradesh

In Visakhapatnam, where we are based, this dish holds a special place. Considered a gourmet delicacy, it is made with ghee and reserved for special occasions. Known as MLA Pesarattu, it is said to have earned its name after the release of a Telugu movie titled *MLA Pesarattu*.

I vividly remember my father painstakingly preparing this dish whenever guests visited. His meticulous effort and dedication made it a memorable experience for everyone who had the pleasure of tasting it.

PESARATTU UPMA
(Savoury Moong Dal Dosa with Flavourful Upma)

SUPRIYA DEVERKONDA — ANDHRA PRADESH

SERVES: 4 — PREPARATION TIME: 6–8 HOURS

COOK TIME: 30–45 MINUTES

INGREDIENTS

FOR PESARATTU:

Split moong dal/green whole moong dal	100 gms

Dhuli moong dal	100 gms
Ginger paste	½ tbsp
Oil (sesame oil preferred)	60 ml
Onions	2, finely chopped
Green chillies	1–2 chopped
Cumin seeds	1 tsp
Salt	to taste

FOR UPMA:

Sooji (semolina)	200 gms
Water	400 ml
Onion	1, finely chopped
Ginger	10–15 gms
Green chillies	1–2, finely chopped
Mustard seeds	1–2 tsp
Chana dal	1–2 tsp
Curry leaves	4–6
Cashews	10–15, broken
Salt	to taste
Desi ghee	1 tbsp

METHOD

Soak the split moong dal and dhuli moong dal overnight in water, preferably for 6–8 hours. The soak time can be reduced in the summer months to 4–5 hours.

Drain the soaked dal and grind it into a smooth paste with ginger, cumin seeds, salt, and green chillies. The batter for Pesarattu is ready.

In a separate pan, roast the sooji until it is slightly brown and keep it aside.

Now, take a kadhai, heat desi ghee in it, and add chana dal. Fry till it turns slightly brown. Then, add cashews and continue to fry until they are also slightly browned.

Add mustard seeds and let them splutter. Then, add the green chillies, ginger, and curry leaves.

Add the chopped onions and sauté until they turn golden brown.

Separately, heat water until it comes to a boil. (This step ensures quicker cooking; a trick I learned from my mother.)

Add the boiling water to the kadhai with the tempering and onions. Stir in salt to taste.

Slowly add the sooji, stirring continuously to prevent lumps.

Cook for 10–15 minutes on medium heat, stirring occasionally, until the upma reaches the desired consistency. For a drier upma, cook a little longer.

Now, heat a dosa tawa (griddle). Sprinkle a little water to check if it is hot—the water should sizzle and evaporate quickly.

Lightly grease the tawa with oil. Pour a ladleful of the ground pesarattu batter onto the tawa and spread it in a circular motion, like a dosa. Sprinkle chopped onions and green chillies evenly on top of the batter.

Once the bottom is slightly brown, flip the pesarattu and let it cook for 1–2 minutes. Then, flip it back.

Spread a layer of the prepared upma on the side of the pesarattu where the onions were added. Fold the pesarattu over the upma.

Serving suggestion: Serve the Pesarattu Upma hot with coconut chutney or chutney powder.

Note: The freshly ground batter can be used to prepare pesarattu right after grinding and does not require fermentation.

If you prefer a slightly wet consistency of the upma, increase the water quantity to 800 ml.

Dry Vegetables

Masala Arbi

by Chitra Agarwal, Uttar Pradesh

I have always been fond of cooking and take great pride in having hosted parties for up to sixty people, cooking everything myself with only the support of my family. I enjoy experimenting with various cuisines—whether it's Chinese, South Indian, Continental, or others—and love feeding healthy, home-cooked meals to my children and, now, my grandchildren.

Whenever my daughters faced difficulties in getting their kids to eat a particular vegetable, it was always Nani to the rescue. So, when my younger daughter struggled to get her son to eat arbi (taro root), I took on the challenge. I pulled out one of my age-old, handed-down-the-generations, simple yet flavourful Masala Arbi recipes and paired it with a paratha.

To my delight, my grandson fell in love with the dish that very day and ate it even without the paratha. He still loves it and affectionately calls it 'Nani wali arbi'!

MASALA ARBI
(Spiced Taro Root)

CHITRA AGARWAL — UTTAR PRADESH

SERVES: 2 — PREPARATION TIME: 10 MINUTES

COOK TIME: 20 MINUTES

INGREDIENTS

Arbi (taro root)	250 gms
Asafoetida	a pinch
Carom seeds	½ tsp
Cumin seeds	½ tsp
Cumin powder	1 tsp, roasted
Coriander powder	½ tbsp
Fennel powder	½ tsp
Red chilli powder	½ tsp
Green chillies	2, slit longitudinally
Salt	to taste
Amchoor (dry mango powder)	1½ tbsp
Chaat masala	½ tsp
Lemon juice (optional)	1 tsp
Mustard oil	4 tbsp
Coriander leaves	chopped, to garnish
Water	200 ml (approx.)

METHOD

Wash the arbi well and boil it whole in a pressure cooker with 200 ml of water until it releases 2 whistles.

Once boiled, peel the arbi and cut into 1 cm thick roundels.

In a pan, heat mustard oil till it starts to smoke. Allow it to cool a little (this is important to prevent the masalas from burning), and then add asafoetida, carom seeds, and cumin seeds. Let them splutter.

Add the green chillies, roasted cumin powder, coriander powder, fennel powder, red chilli powder, and salt. Roast the spices together for 2–3 minutes.

Then, add the arbi roundels and toss gently to coat them with the masalas. Avoid stirring it vigorously to prevent mashing the arbi.

Cook the arbi on low flame for 10 minutes, tossing occasionally. If you prefer a crisper texture, cook for a little longer.

Finally, sprinkle dry mango powder, chaat masala, and pour a bit of lemon juice (if you like) over the arbi. Toss everything together lightly to coat the arbi well, making sure not to break or crush it.

To garnish, add freshly chopped coriander leaves and enjoy your Masala Arbi!

Serving suggestion: Masala Arbi can be relished with parathas, pooris, rotis, or even as a snack on its own.

Note: Be careful not to overcook the arbi, as it should remain firm and not turn mushy. Boiling the arbi a few hours earlier or even a day in advance helps achieve the best results.

Chakkakuru Mezhukkupuratti

by Sobana Kevin, Kerala

I developed a passion for cooking and experimenting with different culinary styles from a young age. And after my marriage, my mother-in-law introduced me to the cuisine of Kerala. She was an incredible cook who loved preparing traditional dishes that were simple, quick, yet rich in flavour. She taught me this recipe using her favourite iron cookware, insisting it tasted best when cooked in it—and I have to agree. The simplicity of the preparation and the health benefits of jackfruit seeds made it easy for me to learn this recipe.

To this day, my son fondly calls this recipe Ammumma's chakkakuru. Every time I make it, the memories of my mother-in-law and me spending time together fill my heart with happiness. This recipe truly holds a special place in both my heart and my family's.

CHAKKAKURU MEZHUKKUPURATTI
(Stir-fried Jackfruit Seeds)

SOBANA KEVIN | KERALA

SERVES: 4 | PREPARATION TIME: 20 MINUTES

COOK TIME: 20 MINUTES

INGREDIENTS

Jackfruit seeds	200 gms
Pearl onions/Button onions	16, sliced
Garlic	4 cloves, finely chopped
Kashmiri red chilli powder	½ tsp
Black pepper powder	¼ tsp
Curry leaves	1 sprig
Fresh coconut	30 gms, grated
Mustard seeds	½ tsp
Coconut oil	2 tbsp
Salt	to taste

METHOD

Add the jackfruit seeds in a pressure cooker and pour enough water to just submerge them. Cook them until the cooker releases 3 whistles.

The seeds should retain a slight bite when done. If the seeds are still undercooked, cook them for 1 or 2 more whistles. It is important not to overcook the seeds, as they may become mushy. Once cooked, allow the pressure to release naturally. Drain off the excess water.

Peel off the outer covering of the jackfruit seeds, which should come out easily if cooked to the right temperature. Now slice the seeds into thin slivers.

Heat a cast iron kadhai or handi over a medium flame.

Add coconut oil to the kadhai. Once warmed, add mustard

seeds and curry leaves. Wait for the mustard seeds to splutter.

Then, add the chopped garlic, sliced pearl onions, Kashmiri red chilli powder, and black pepper powder in the tempering.

Now, add the thinly slivered jackfruit seeds and sauté them until they are well-coated with the masalas.

Turn off the flame and stir in the grated fresh coconut. Mix well, and the dish is ready to serve.

Serving suggestion: Enjoy Chakkakuru Mezhukkupuratti with Kerala-style Kanji.

Gunda Kachri ki Sabzi
by Abhilasha Jain, Rajasthan

As I am from a Marwari household, certain flavours instantly transport me back to childhood, evoking memories of family gatherings, festivals, and the comforting aroma of home-cooked meals. One such dish is Gunda Kachri ki Sabzi—a dish that carries the essence of Rajasthan's rustic charm and the simplicity and warmth of family ties. For many, gunda (or lasoda) and kachri are not just ingredients; they embody a tradition passed down through generations.

I remember my grandmother meticulously preparing this sabzi with such rhythm, honed through years of experience. She would often tell us stories of how she learned the recipe from her mother, who had learned it from hers.

Each bite of the sabzi was a connection to our roots, a taste of the land our ancestors called home. The tangy, slightly bitter taste of gunda, combined with the earthy spiciness of kachri, creates a symphony of unique Rajasthani flavours. It's a dish that speaks of resilience, of making the most of the arid land and turning it into something extraordinary.

Preparing Gunda Kachri ki Sabzi isn't just about cooking; it's about preserving a legacy. It's about remembering the hands that taught us, the stories that were shared around the kitchen fire, and the love that was infused into every meal. As I make this sabzi today, I am reminded of the times spent with my grandmother, learning not just how to cook but how to keep our traditions alive.

GUNDA KACHRI KI SABZI
(Glueberry and Wild Melon Curry)

ABHILASHA JAIN — RAJASTHAN

SERVES: 5 — PREPARATION TIME: 2 HOURS

COOK TIME: 45 MINUTES

INGREDIENTS

Ingredient	Quantity
Gunda/Lasoda (glueberry)	200 gms
Kachri (wild melon)	100 gms, dried and crushed
Groundnut oil	2 tbsp
Cumin seeds	1 tsp
Mustard seeds	1 tsp
Asafoetida	1/4 tsp
Green chillies	2–3, slit longitudinally
Turmeric powder	1 tsp
Red chilli powder	1 tsp
Coriander powder	1 tsp
Amchoor (dry mango powder)	1 tsp
Water	500 ml (approx.)
Salt	to taste
Coriander leaves	chopped, to garnish

METHOD

To prepare the gunda, wash it thoroughly. Slit each one of them.

Bring a pot of water to a boil, add a pinch of salt, and parboil the gunda for about 5–7 minutes until slightly tender. Drain and set aside.

Soak the crushed kachri in warm water for 15–20 minutes to soften it. Then, drain the water and keep it aside.

For tempering, heat groundnut oil in a heavy-bottomed pan until it starts to smoke. Lower the heat and add cumin seeds, mustard seeds, and asafoetida. Once the seeds crackle, add the slit green chillies and sauté for a minute.

Now, add the parboiled gunda to the pan and sauté for 5–7 minutes on medium heat until they turn golden.

Add turmeric powder, red chilli powder, coriander powder, and salt to season the mixture. Stir well to coat the gunda with the spices.

Add the soaked kachri to the pan. Mix everything and cook for another 10–15 minutes on low heat, stirring occasionally.

For the final touch, sprinkle dry mango powder over the sabzi and give it a stir. This adds a bit of a tanginess that balances the flavours.

Garnish with chopped coriander leaves and serve hot.

Serving suggestion: Gunda Kachri ki Sabzi pairs beautifully with bajra roti or even with plain phulkas. A side of curd or buttermilk complements the meal, making it a wholesome experience.

Curries

Amti
by Anuradha Walia, Maharashtra

Amti is a popular arhar dal dish from Maharashtra that holds a special place in my heart. My nana, who grew up in Kolhapur, was especially fond of it. When my nani and nana moved to Delhi, my great-grandmother shared the recipe with my nani, who then passed it down to my mother.

Coming from a Baniya family, where the sweet and tangy flavours of Amti were not typically enjoyed, the dish was rarely made. Similarly, after marrying into a Punjabi family, Amti didn't initially gain much popularity. However, the distinct taste of this dal lingered in my memory, and I soon realized what I had been missing. So, I began making it for myself. To my delight, my Punjabi family has come to love it as well.

In keeping with tradition, I now look forward to passing down this recipe to my daughter and daughter-in-law, ensuring that Amti remains a cherished part of our family's culinary heritage.

AMTI
(Tangy, Sweet, and Spicy Lentil Curry)

ANURADHA WALIA | MAHARASHTRA

SERVES: 4 | PREPARATION TIME: 1 HOUR 15 MINUTES

COOK TIME: 25 MINUTES

INGREDIENTS

Toor/Arhar dal (split pigeon peas)	200 gms
Tamarind	2 big pieces
Red chillies	2
Cumin seeds	1½ tsp
Coriander seeds	1½ tsp
Coconut	1½ tsp, grated
Turmeric powder	½ tsp
Jaggery	2 tsp, powdered
Desi ghee	2 tbsp
Mustard seeds	½ tsp
Asafoetida	¼ tsp
Red chilli powder	¼ tsp
Curry leaves	8–10
Coriander leaves	chopped, to garnish
Salt	to taste
Water	450 ml (approx.)

METHOD

Rinse the arhar dal thoroughly. Soak it in 400 ml of water for an hour.

Now, soak tamarind in 50 ml of lukewarm water for 10 minutes and extract the pulp.

Take a pan and dry roast the cumin seeds, coriander seeds, grated coconut, and whole red chillies. Let them cool, and then grind them into a powder.

Pour the soaked arhar dal along with the water into a pressure cooker. Add some salt and turmeric powder to it, and cook until the pressure cooker releases 2 whistles.

Open the cooker and stir in the tamarind pulp, roasted ground powder, and jaggery powder. Cook the dal for another minute on medium heat.

For the tempering, heat desi ghee in a pan. Once hot, add the asafoetida, mustard seeds, curry leaves, and red chilli powder, and allow them to splutter. Pour this over the cooked dal.

Garnish with fresh coriander leaves and serve.

Serving suggestion: Serve it hot with steamed rice.

Kacchi Haldi ki Sabzi
by Deepti Bhatnagar, Rajasthan

I come from Jodhpur, Rajasthan, a region renowned for its vibrant culture and indulgent use of desi ghee. One dish that holds a special place in my heart is Kacchi Haldi ki Sabzi.

Before I got married, I would often help my maa prepare this dish, and by the end of it, my hands would turn completely yellow. I loved it when she'd jokingly say, 'Mere haath peele ho gaye,' a comment which would always give me butterflies. Maa would even playfully add, 'Jaldi kara do peele….'

Now, whenever I make this sabzi, my son teases me with, 'Mummy, aapke haath phir se peele ho gaye.'

KACCHI HALDI KI SABZI
(Raw Turmeric Curry)

DEEPTI BHATNAGAR — RAJASTHAN

SERVES: 4 — PREPARATION TIME: 20 MINUTES

COOK TIME: 20 MINUTES

INGREDIENTS

Raw turmeric	200 gms, washed, peeled, and grated
Onion	1, big, chopped

Ginger	3-inch piece, washed, peeled, and grated
Garlic	8–9 cloves, chopped
Curd	½ cup, at room temperature
Desi ghee	½ cup
Cumin seeds	1 tsp
Peas	½ cup
Tomatoes	2, finely chopped
Salt	to taste
Red chilli powder	to taste
Coriander powder	½–1 tsp
Garam masala powder	1 tsp
Coriander leaves	chopped, to garnish
Cashews (optional)	10–12, fried
Water	100 ml

METHOD

Heat desi ghee in a kadhai. Add cumin seeds and let them crackle. Then, add grated raw turmeric and fry for 5–6 minutes.

Mix in grated ginger, chopped onions, and chopped garlic cloves. Sauté the mixture for 2–3 minutes until aromatic.

Add red chilli powder and coriander powder, and sauté for another minute.

Now, add the tomatoes and cook for 3–4 minutes until they soften.

Add green peas, 100 ml of water, and salt to taste. Cover and cook on low flame till the peas are tender and everything is well cooked.

Beat the curd until smooth. Lower the flame and add the curd to the kadhai, stirring continuously to prevent it from splitting. Cover and cook for another 5–6 minutes.

Sprinkle some garam masala powder and freshly chopped coriander leaves.

Your sabzi is now ready to serve! You can also garnish it with fried cashews.

Serving suggestion: Kacchi Haldi ki Sabzi pairs well with Khoba Roti or hot parathas.

Pittor in Curd Gravy
by Payal Nandwana, Rajasthan

My grandfather was a true foodie, especially when it came to dishes made with besan—a trait that has been passed down to me. I have fond memories from my childhood, watching my mom prepare a variety of besan-based recipes, and one of my favourites was Pittor in Curd Gravy. I loved the way she made it.

Sadly, I never had the chance to learn the exact measurements from her, as she passed away unexpectedly. For a long time, I yearned to recreate that same taste but struggled to find the exact recipe. After numerous attempts and countless trials, I think I have finally succeeded. Now, I'm thrilled to share that very recipe with you.

PITTOR IN CURD GRAVY
(Chickpea Flour Dumplings in Yogurt Gravy)

PAYAL NANDWANA — RAJASTHAN

SERVES: 5–6

PREPARATION TIME: 15 MINUTES

COOK TIME: 30 MINUTES

INGREDIENTS

FOR PITTOR:

Besan (chickpea flour)	250 gms
Water	550 ml
Salt	1 tsp
Turmeric powder	½ tsp
Red chilli powder	½ tsp
Carom seeds	¼ tsp

FOR GRAVY:

Oil	1 tbsp
Cumin seeds	½ tsp
Asafoetida	⅛ tsp or a pinch
Green chillies	1–2, finely chopped
Curry leaves	10–12
Coriander powder	2 tsp
Red chilli powder	2 tsp or to taste
Turmeric powder	1 tsp
Water	2 ltrs
Sour curd	250 ml, blended at room temperature
Salt	2 tsp or to taste
Garam masala powder	1 tsp
Coriander leaves	chopped, to garnish

METHOD

Pittor

Take besan and sieve it to remove any lumps. In a wok, add besan, salt, red chilli powder, turmeric powder, and carom seeds. Gradually add water while stirring continuously to ensure no lumps are formed.

Turn on the stove. Place the wok over it and cook it for 6–7 minutes, stirring continuously. The besan will thicken as it cooks. To check if it's ready, take half a teaspoon of cooked besan, flatten it on a plate, and try to lift it with your finger. If it comes off easily without sticking, it's done.

Quickly, spread this besan in a thin layer on a large flat plate or the back of the plate. Allow it to cool and dry for a few minutes.

Once dried, cut the besan layer into small cubes or diamond-shaped pieces. Pittor is ready.

Gravy

Heat oil in a wok, add asafoetida and cumin seeds. Let them splutter. Add green chillies and curry leaves. Sauté briefly.

In a bowl, mix red chilli powder, coriander powder, and turmeric powder with some water. Gently add this mixture to the prepared tempering and stir well. Add more water to it and bring it to a boil, cooking for 5–6 minutes.

Now, add the blended curd and keep stirring till it starts boiling. Let it boil for 2–3 minutes.

Gently add the prepared pittor pieces to this gravy and let the mixture simmer for 2–3 minutes.

Finally, add salt and garam masala.

Garnish with fresh chopped coriander leaves.

Serving suggestion: Serve it hot with plain parathas or rotis. Dry Pittor can also be fried and served as snacks.

Note: Adding salt at the end helps thicken the gravy. Adjust the consistency with more water as needed.

Sindhi Kadhi
by Priyanka Talreja, Sindh

My family hails from Shikarpur, now part of Karachi, Pakistan. Growing up in a true Sindhi household, Sunday lunches were incomplete without Sindhi Kadhi with chawal and Aloo ke Tuk. It was a cherished staple throughout my childhood. My dad and I loved this simple yet soulful dish so much that we would often enjoy mugful of kadhi even before lunchtime.

My mom passed away when I was 18, and I didn't know how to cook. It was my maasi, who lived in another city, who taught me all the traditional Sindhi recipes. She was my personal YouTube channel—quite literally—as she patiently explained each step over the phone to ensure I didn't make any mistakes.

Every time I make this Sindhi Kadhi, it feels like a warm hug from my loved ones and takes me back to my childhood.

SINDHI KADHI
(Tangy-Spicy Chickpea Flour Curry with Assorted Vegetables)

PRIYANKA TALREJA | SINDH

SERVES: 4 | PREPARATION TIME: 15 MINUTES

COOK TIME: 45 MINUTES

INGREDIENTS

Tomatoes	10, medium-sized
Water	1 ltr
Bhindi (okra)	8–10
Refined oil	250 ml
Drumsticks	2
Desi ghee	4 tbsp
Mustard seeds	½ tsp
Fenugreek seeds	½ tsp
Cumin seeds	½ tsp
Besan (chickpea flour)	35 gms
Asafoetida	1 tsp
Curry leaves	10–12
Kashmiri red chilli powder	1 tsp
Cluster beans	10–12
Dried kokum flowers	5–6
Ginger	2 tbsp, chopped
Green chillies	4, slit longitudinally
Salt	to taste
Coriander leaves	to garnish

METHOD

Pressure cook 10 tomatoes with 1 litre of water for 3–4 whistles. Once the pressure releases, blend the tomatoes using a hand blender. Strain it using a sieve and set the liquid aside.

Peel the drumsticks, and cut them into small, finger-sized pieces.

Ensure that the okra is completely dry and make a vertical slit halfway through the centre. Deep fry the okra pieces in oil (or air fry, if preferred) and keep aside.

In a wide, heavy-bottomed pan, heat 4 tablespoons of desi ghee. Add fenugreek seeds, mustard seeds, and cumin seeds, and let them splutter.

Reduce the flame to the lowest setting, add besan, and stir continuously with a rubber spatula to avoid burning. Roast the besan until it turns medium-dark brown and fragrant, which might take about 15 minutes.

Once the besan is roasted, add asafoetida, red chilli powder, curry leaves. Stir for 30 seconds.

Then, add the drumsticks and cluster beans, stir for 2 minutes, and pour in a glass full of cold water. Mix well to avoid any lumps. Add the prepared tomato liquid to the chickpea flour gravy.

Now, add chopped ginger, slit green chillies, 5–6 pieces of dried kokum flowers, salt, and let the kadhi come to a rolling boil.

Once it starts boiling, add the deep-fried okra pieces, reduce the flame to medium-low, cover the pan with a lid, and let it boil for at least 30 minutes or until the desi ghee begins to float on top.

Serving suggestion: Garnish with lots of freshly chopped coriander leaves and serve hot with steamed rice.

Note: One tablespoon tamarind pulp can be used as a substitute to dried kokum flowers for the tanginess.

Doi Begun

by Sumita Basu Banerjee, West Bengal

Doi Begun is a popular dish in India, and it's fascinating how every region prepares it with its own unique blend of spices, making it taste different wherever you go. Begun or brinjal, as it's known in most places, has an interesting name in Bangla—'Bay-Goon', which humorously means 'someone with no qualities'. But jokes aside, brinjal is a highly nutritious vegetable, packed with fibre, vitamins, minerals, and a lot of antioxidants, all while being low in calories. When cooked with the right mix of spices, it can rival any non-vegetarian dish in taste.

As a child, I was quite the fussy eater, giving my mother and grandmother a tough time. Now, as a mother myself, I understand what it's like to always be on the front lines, battling to get your kids to eat well. They would make dishes that were not only nutritious and healthy, but also delicious—and Doi Begun was one of them.

The best brinjals come in winter, but if you love this vegetable, no season will stop you from enjoying it. With just a few ingredients, this dish can be so delicious! My son always says, 'tastes like heaven, Maa!'

DOI BEGUN
(Eggplant in Yogurt Sauce)

SUMITA BASU BANERJEE

WEST BENGAL

SERVES: 4

PREPARATION TIME: 1 HOUR 15 MINUTES (INCLUDING 1 HOUR OF MARINATION)

COOK TIME: 10 MINUTES

INGREDIENTS

Brinjals	8, small (around 400 gms)
Yogurt	200 gms
Panch Phoron (five spice mix)	1 tbsp
Dry red chillies (whole)	2
Asafoetida	½ tbsp
Ginger, garlic, green chilli	2 tbsp, coarse paste
Kashmiri red chilli powder	1 tbsp
Sugar	2 tbsp
Salt	to taste
Wheat flour	2 tbsp
Curry leaves	8–10 leaves
Coriander leaves	chopped, to garnish
Mustard oil	2 tbsp
Refined oil	to deep fry the brinjals
Water	200 ml

FOR PANCH PHORON:

Cumin seeds	1 tbsp
Kalonji/kala jeera (nigella seeds)	1 tbsp
Fennel seeds	2 tbsp
Fenugreek seeds	3 tbsp
Mustard seeds	½ tbsp

METHOD

Wash the brinjals and slit them lengthwise into four parts, keeping them intact at the stem.

Smear 1 tablespoon of salt evenly on both the outside and inside of the brinjals, and gently rub it in.

Transfer the brinjals to a steel colander, with a plate underneath to store any water. Cover them and set aside for 1 to 2 hours to drain.

After 2 hours, take a kadhai and deep fry the brinjals in refined oil, until their outer shells look crispy. Ensure the inside is cooked properly. They should be light brown in colour.

In a large bowl, add yogurt, ginger-garlic-green chilli paste, Kashmiri red chilli powder, wheat flour, salt, and sugar. Mix well, ensuring there are no lumps. Gradually, add water to get a thinner consistency, then cover and keep aside.

For making the panch phoron, mix the ingredients listed.

(You will need only 1 tbsp of the panch phoron for this recipe. You can store the rest in an airtight container for use in other dishes like sabzi or dal tadka.)

Take another large kadhai and heat mustard oil in it. Add whole red chillies, panch phoron, and curry leaves. Let them splutter.

Turn off the flame, and add asafoetida.

Pour the yogurt mixture into this tempering and stir vigorously until well combined.

Continue cooking the mixture over low heat until you see oil floating on the top.

Add the fried brinjals and simmer over medium heat for another 5 minutes.

Garnish with chopped coriander leaves, then cover the kadhai and let it sit for 3 minutes before serving.

Serving suggestion: Serve it hot with steamed rice, roti, or paratha.

Note: The brinjals can be shallow-fried in less oil or even in an air fryer for a healthier version. It is completely optional.

Kacche Ambh di Mahni
by Priyanka Rajpal, Punjab

This recipe holds a special place in my heart, not only for its rich, tangy-sweet flavours, but also because it's a true heirloom, passed down through generations in our family. My baba (grandfather) taught my mother how to make Kacche Ambh di Mahni, a distinctive Punjabi mango curry that blends the sharpness of raw green mangoes with a subtle sweetness, creating a harmony of flavours that dance on the palate. What made this dish even more special was Baba's insistence on including the guthli (mango seed), a nod to his belief that nothing should ever go to waste.

Baba often reminisced about his time in pre-partition Pakistan, sharing stories of foraging for fallen kacche ambh (raw mangoes) after unseasonal summer rains. These small, yet incredibly juicy mangoes, which might otherwise have been discarded, were transformed by Baba into this delightful dish. He would always highlight that even the tiniest mangoes were rich with gooda (flesh), a testament to the abundance of the land he came from.

In Punjabi households, food is more than just sustenance—it's the heartbeat of the home, the thread that weaves generations together. This dish, in particular, is a treasure trove of memories. Baba knew mangoes were my favourite, and he would lovingly prepare this curry just for me, filling the kitchen with its mouth-watering aroma.

Now, I carry on this tradition with my daughter. Although we live in Australia, where raw mangoes can be hard to find, we savour every bite of 'guthli wali mahni' whenever we manage to get them from the Indian grocery store. It's a rare treat, a taste of home and heritage, linking us to the past while creating new memories for the future.

KACCHE AMBH DI MAHNI
(Raw Mango Sweet and Sour Relish)

PRIYANKA RAJPAL | PUNJAB

SERVES: 4 | PREPARATION TIME: 10 MINUTES

COOK TIME: 10 MINUTES

INGREDIENTS

Raw mangoes	8–10, small-sized
Mustard oil	2 tbsp
Cumin seeds	1 tsp
Fennel seeds	2 tsp, crushed
Kalonji (nigella seeds)	1 tsp
Coriander seeds	1 tsp, crushed
Turmeric powder	1 tsp
Red chilli powder	1 tsp
Jaggery	2 tbsp, powdered
Green chillies	2, slit in half
Salt	to taste
Water	450 ml

METHOD

Wash and peel the raw mangoes. Cook them in a pressure cooker with some water until it releases 1 whistle. Let the pressure release naturally. Remove the mangoes and extract their pulp, making sure to retain the seeds and the cooking water.

Heat oil in a kadhai. Add the cumin seeds and let them splutter. Then, add green chillies and the remaining spices like turmeric powder, red chilli powder, coriander seeds, fennel seeds, and kalonji.

To prevent the spices from burning, add a tablespoon of water and sauté briefly.

Now, add the boiled mango pulp, the seeds, and the stored water.

Stir in jaggery and salt as per taste (ensuring the relish keeps a balance of sweet, sour, and salty), and cook until the mahni thickens slightly.

Serving suggestion: Serve it hot with rice, roti, or paratha.

Note: Sugar can be used as a substitute for jaggery. However, jaggery imparts a rich golden-brown colour to the mahni.

Chicken

Chicken Pulao

by Shefali Saxena, Lahore

This simple recipe was passed down from my father-in-law, who was an exceptional cook. His culinary skills were deeply rooted in Lahori cuisine, a legacy from his family's time in Lahore before they moved to Delhi after Partition. Specializing in mutton dishes, he was renowned for his exceptional Mutton Pulao. However, when chicken eaters were present, he would adapt his recipe into this delicious Chicken Pulao.

Though my daughter was very young when we lost him, his Chicken Pulao is her favourite meal. It's the one dish she's eager to learn before heading abroad for her future studies.

CHICKEN PULAO
(One-pot Chicken Rice)

SHEFALI SAXENA	LAHORE
SERVES: 3–4	PREPARATION TIME: 1 HOUR
	COOK TIME: 45 MINUTES

INGREDIENTS

Chicken	500 gms (preferably leg/thigh pieces)
Basmati rice	300 gms

Black cardamom	3
Green cardamom	5
Bay leaves	2
Cinnamon	2 sticks
Cloves	8
Whole black pepper	1 tbsp
Ginger-garlic paste	1 tbsp
Desi ghee	2 tbsp
Ginger	2-inch piece, sliced in thin slivers
Onions	2, big, sliced
Green chillies (optional)	2, slit longitudinally
Potatoes (optional)	2, medium-sized
Lemon juice	½ lemon
Garam masala/Chicken masala	2 tbsp
Chilli powder	to taste
Salt	to taste
Water	500 ml

FOR THE MARINADE:

Ginger-garlic paste	1 tbsp
Plain curd	3 tbsp, thick
Lemon juice	½ lemon
Garam masala/Chicken masala	1 tsp
Salt	to taste
Red chilli powder	to taste

FOR GARNISHING:

Mint leaves	3–4 sprigs
Onion	1, large, sliced
Oil	to fry
Eggs (optional)	2, boiled

METHOD

Mix all the marinade ingredients and coat the chicken pieces well. Let the chicken marinate for at least 1 hour.

Soak the rice in water for 30 minutes. Keep it aside. Remember to drain the water later.

Slice 1 large onion and deep fry in oil or ghee until brown. Drain the fried onions on a paper towel to remove excess oil. Set aside for garnishing.

If using, boil and peel the eggs.

Peel the potatoes, if using, and prick them all over with a fork.

Now, in a kadhai, heat desi ghee. Add the whole masalas like black cardamom, green cardamom, bay leaves, cinnamon, cloves, and whole black pepper and sauté for a few seconds until fragrant. Then put the onions and sauté until they turn golden brown. (They don't need to be crisped fully.)

Add ginger-garlic paste and marinated chicken (along with potatoes, if using), and fry till the chicken is browned.

Add the garam masala or chicken masala, salt, chilli powder, lemon juice, ginger slivers, green chillies, and 500 ml of water. Drain the pre-soaked rice and add it to the mixture. Bring the mixture to a boil, cover the pan, and cook on a low flame until the rice is cooked and the flavours are well combined.

Once done, garnish with mint leaves, top the dish with fried onions, and add sliced boiled eggs (if using).

Serving suggestion: Serve hot with mint or garlic raita.

Dahi Methi Murgh

by Anshu Bhatia, Punjab

In our family kitchen, there's one dish that holds a cherished place in our hearts—Dahi Methi Murgh. It is a dish that embodies the warmth of tradition, the comfort of home, and the flavours of generations past. This simple yet rich delight was passed down through the years, from my dad to me, and now to my daughter. This heirloom recipe, lovingly learned by my dad from his family, is a testament to the beauty of simplicity. With just a handful of ingredients, it creates a burst of flavours that dance on your taste buds.

I still remember the anticipation and excitement that filled the air whenever Dad announced he'd be making Dahi Methi Murgh. The aroma of spices mingling with yogurt and fenugreek leaves would waft through the house, drawing us all to the kitchen like moths to a flame. Dad would work his magic with the ingredients, carefully measuring each one and adding them to the simmering pot. There was something almost poetic in the way he cooked—each stir felt like a rhythm, each step a melody. I would watch him, mesmerized, trying to memorize every detail, every secret of this treasured recipe.

Though I've made a few improvisations here and there, just a little tweak to add my own touch, the essence of the recipe remains untouched—a tribute to my dad's culinary legacy. Now, whenever I prepare Dahi Methi Murgh, it's not just about the food—it's about the memories it brings back, the connection to my roots, and the joy it brings to my family, especially my daughter. She loves this dish as much as I did when my dad used to make it for us.

Dahi Methi Murgh is a flavourful journey through time, a reminder of where we come from, and a celebration of the love that binds our family together. And as I pass this recipe on to my daughter, I know that this legacy will continue to bring joy to our family for many years to come.

DAHI METHI MURGH
(Chicken in Yogurt and Dried Fenugreek Sauce)

ANSHU BHATIA — PUNJAB

SERVES: 4 — PREPARATION TIME: 2–3 HOURS

COOK TIME: 45–60 MINUTES

INGREDIENTS

Curd	200 gms
Ginger paste	1 tbsp
Garlic paste	1 tbsp
Red chilli powder	1 tsp
Turmeric powder	1 tsp
Coriander powder	1 tsp
Chicken masala powder	1tsp
Salt	to taste
Chicken	1 kg, drumsticks or whole chicken cut into medium pieces
Oil	2 tbsp
Cumin seeds	1 tsp
Onions	3–4, medium-sized, ground to paste
Salt	to taste

Kasoori methi (dried fenugreek leaves)	1 tbsp
Water	250 ml (approx.)

METHOD

To marinate the chicken, coat it with curd, ginger paste, garlic paste, turmeric powder, red chilli powder, coriander powder, chicken masala powder, and salt. Keep it in the refrigerator for 2–3 hours.

Heat 2 tablespoons of oil in a kadhai. Add cumin seeds, and once they splutter, add the onion paste. Sauté until golden brown.

Add the marinated chicken to the kadhai and cook on high flame for 2–3 minutes.

Pour in around 250 ml of water and bring to a boil. Add salt to taste.

Now, cover the kadhai with a lid and cook the chicken on medium flame. Stir occasionally and add more water if required. Cook until the chicken becomes tender.

Just before turning off the flame, crush the kasoori methi with your palms and sprinkle it over the chicken.

Serving suggestion: Serve hot with rice, roti, or paratha.

Photey Mein Chicken
by Upasana Mahtani, Sindh

I'm deeply passionate about preserving Sindhi recipes for my children, as I worry that a few years from now, our rich heritage might fade away. To keep these traditions alive, I recreate recipes as I remember them, blending the old with my own personal touches.

There's an old family cook of ours who makes Photey Mein Chicken, taught to him by a Sindhi aunt. My dear cousin has her own version as well. During the pandemic, I suddenly recalled this recipe. I immediately called my mom, as she is the treasure trove of all our family recipes, and she guided me through the steps, just as she used to do when I was younger. Since then, I've made it several times, tweaking it here and there until it became an excellent addition to any meal. This recipe is a collaboration of the original and what works best for me.

I often think back to the times I would ask my grandmother about the nuances of recipes, and this dish seems to be a product of those conversations. In Sindhi, 'photta' refers to elaichi or cardamom. Hence, this dish can be made with either chicken or mutton. The gravy is thin and light, designed to soothe when someone is unwell. While there are many variations of this dish, I prefer this particular one, especially for the addition of spinach leaves.

PHOTEY MEIN CHICKEN
(Chicken and Spinach Curry)

UPASANA MAHTANI — SINDH

SERVES: 3–4

PREPARATION TIME: 15 MINUTES

COOK TIME: 45 MINUTES

INGREDIENTS

Chicken leg pieces	4
Boneless chicken	500 gms
Red tomatoes	3, pureed
Green chillies (optional)	5–6, pureed
Green cardamom	5–6, crushed coarsely with skins
Coriander powder	1 tsp
Salt	1 tsp
Black peppercorns	1 tsp, crushed
Whole wheat flour	1 tbsp
Water	100 ml
Spinach leaves	100 gms

METHOD

Wash and clean the chicken pieces.

In a pressure cooker, heat oil and add the crushed cardamom pods (with the skin). Add the chicken pieces and cook for 7–8 minutes.

Add 1 tsp each of salt, crushed black pepper, and coriander powder.

Add the pureed tomatoes and cook for a few minutes, until the raw smell of the tomatoes is gone.

If you prefer a little heat, add pureed green chillies as well.

Add some water to the cooker, close the lid, and cook for 2 whistles, ensuring the contents do not stick to the bottom.

After opening the cooker, add 100 ml of water with 1 tablespoon of whole wheat flour to thicken the gravy.

Add spinach leaves to the cooker and cover it again. The spinach will cook in the residual heat.

Garnish with a sprinkling of freshly ground black pepper and serve hot.

Murgh Chole

by Nancy Singh, Punjab

In most north Indian homes, chicken curry and chole are more than just dishes—they are an emotion. A bowl of curry served with rice or chapati is a beloved staple for lunch or dinner.

The aroma of spices blending with the nutritious chickpeas and tender chicken evokes cherished memories of my mom's kitchen. This unique combination, a childhood favourite, hails from the fertile lands of Punjab and Sindh (now part of a neighbouring country).

My love for this recipe was passed down from my mom, and now, my daughter loves it so much that I'm sure she will pass on the recipe to the next generation.

MURGH CHOLE
(Chicken and Chickpea Curry)

NANCY SINGH — PUNJAB

SERVES: 3–4 — PREPARATION TIME: 30 MINUTES

COOK TIME: 1 HOUR

INGREDIENTS

Chicken	400 gms, with bone
Chickpeas	200 gms, boiled

Mustard oil/Desi ghee	100 ml
Onions	2, large
Tomatoes	2
Bay leaf	1
Garlic paste	1½ tsp
Ginger paste	1½ tsp
Salt	1½ tsp or to taste
Cumin seeds	½ tsp
Coriander powder	½ tsp
Turmeric powder	½ tsp
Red chilli powder	1½ to 2 tsp
Garam masala	½ tsp
Black pepper powder	½ tsp
Coriander leaves	50 gms, finely chopped
Green chillies	3–5, finely sliced
Meat masala (optional)	2 tsp
Kasoori methi (optional)	½ tsp
Water	200 ml (approx.)

Whole spices (optional)

Cinnamon	2 x 1" sticks
Star anise	1
Black cardamom	1
Cloves	8–10

METHOD

Dice the onions and tomatoes into small pieces and set them aside.

Take a pan or kadhai and put it on medium-high heat. Add oil once the pan is hot.

Then, add cumin seeds, bay leaf, and whole spices (if using).

Next, add the chopped onions and cook until they start to turn golden brown at the edges.

Add the garlic and ginger pastes and stir for another minute or two.

Then, add salt, red chilli powder, turmeric powder, and coriander powder. Cook the mixture until the raw smell of masala disappears, being careful not to burn the mixture. If it starts to stick, add a tablespoon of water.

Now add the chopped tomatoes and cook until they soften.

Add the chicken pieces and stir-fry for a minute.

Pour in 200 ml of hot water, add the boiled chickpeas, and bring the mixture to a boil. Cover the pan with a lid and let it simmer on low heat for another 25–30 minutes.

Remove the lid and check if the chicken is cooked. Allow it to cook for another 5–10 minutes, depending on how tender you want the chicken.

Adjust the consistency of your gravy by adding more water if necessary, and then add meat masala, garam masala, black pepper powder, green chillies, and kasoori methi (if using).

Garnish with coriander leaves and green chillies.

Serving suggestion: Serve it hot with steamed rice or parathas.

Koraishutir Kochuri, a Bengali luchi stuffed with a delicious, spiced mixture of cooked peas, and served with Aloo Dum.

Gunda Kachri ki Sabzi, a tangy, slightly bitter, and spicy curry from Rajasthan.

Pittor in Curd Gravy, mouth-watering chickpea dumplings in spiced yogurt gravy, topped with fresh coriander.

Sindhi Kadhi, a traditional delicacy of the Sindhi community.

Mutton Dak Bungalow, a slow-cooked mutton curry that carries the flavours of colonial India.

Gosht ke Pasande, succulent mutton strips in a rich, spiced Awadhi gravy, finished with aromatic garnishes.

Chingrir Chodchodi, appetizing prawns with an assortment of vegetables from West Bengal.

Malwani Crab Curry, a savoury seafood dish from Maharashtra with several spices and creamy coconut.

Puli Inji, a sweet and tangy relish from Kerala.

Vankaya Tomato Pachadi, a zesty tomato–brinjal chutney from Andhra Pradesh.

Bhapa Doi, a creamy, steamed Bengali yogurt dessert with a hint of sweetness, delicately infused with cardamom, pistachio, and saffron.

Haldi ki Pinni, a nutritious and healing treat made with turmeric, embodying the timeless flavours of Punjab.

Kesariya Gulab Kheer, a rosy rice pudding with the richness of saffron from Uttar Pradesh.

Puran Poli, a fragrant, lentil-filled sweet flatbread that graces tables during festivities.

Mutton

Kolkata-style Mutton Dum Biryani
by Durba Ray, West Bengal

This heirloom recipe has been passed down through three generations in our family. Originally crafted by my great-grandmother, it has evolved to incorporate modern ingredients, yet, we continue to prepare it traditionally. We still use mortar and pestle to grind the spices and cook the biryani in a copper handi. This iconic dish remains a family favourite, reserved for special occasions and celebrations, and evokes cherished memories of family and friends coming together to savour it. It also upholds the legacy of Kolkata biryani with its mild yet nuanced flavours.

KOLKATA-STYLE MUTTON DUM BIRYANI
(Kolkata-style Mutton Biryani)

DURBA RAY — WEST BENGAL

SERVES: 4 — PREPARATION TIME: 30 MINUTES

COOK TIME: 90 MINUTES

INGREDIENTS

BIRYANI SPICES:

Green cardamom	6–7
Black cardamom	1–2

Clove	1 tsp
Cinnamon	2, 1-inch sticks
Mace	1
Nutmeg	¼
Star anise	1
Cumin seeds	1 tsp
Fennel seeds	1 tsp
Black peppercorns	1 tsp

MUTTON MARINADE:

Mutton	500 gms, with bone
Hung curd	2–3 tbsp
Garlic	1 tsp, crushed
Ginger	1 tsp, grated
Red chilli powder	1 tsp
Kashmiri red chilli powder	½ tsp
Black pepper powder	⅓ tsp
Biryani masala	1 tbsp
Salt	to taste

BIRYANI RICE:

Basmati rice	500 gms
Bay leaf	1
Green cardamom	6–7
Black cardamom	1–2
Cloves	1 tsp
Cinnamon	2, 1-inch sticks
Mace	1
Nutmeg	¼
Cumin seeds	1 tsp
Fennel seeds	1 tsp
Black peppercorns	1 tsp
Desi ghee	few drops
Water	920 ml
Salt	1 tsp or to taste

OTHER INGREDIENTS:

Onions	2, large, thinly-sliced
Potatoes	2–3, medium to large
Hard-boiled eggs	3
Saffron	8–10 strands
Milk	75 ml, warm
Rose essence	2–3 drops
Kewra water	½ tsp
Desi ghee	5–6 tbsp
Bay leaves	10 (for handi layering)
Kneaded dough	for dum cooking

METHOD

Dry roast all the khada masalas (whole spices) under the Biryani Spices category and grind them into a fine powder. This spice mix is known as biryani masala.

In a large bowl, beat hung curd and mix all marinade ingredients (except salt and mutton) to make a smooth paste. Then, add mutton and salt and keep aside for 4–5 hours, or at least 1 hour, to marinate.

Wash and clean the rice, then soak for 30 minutes. Prepare a pouch of muslin cloth, place all the rice ingredients (except rice, salt, ghee, and bay leaf) inside, and seal it well. In a large pot, bring water to a boil with the bay leaf, salt, ghee, and muslin spice bag. Add the soaked rice and cook until it is half done. Drain the water and spread the rice on a flat surface. Discard the bay leaf and muslin spice bag.

Heat 3 tablespoons of ghee in a wok and fry thinly-sliced onions till golden brown.

Add the marinated mutton and continue frying on medium heat for 15 minutes till the meat becomes tender. It is important at this step to keep stirring the meat every few minutes. Next, add the potatoes and continue frying on low flame until the mutton and potatoes are almost done. Finally, add the boiled eggs and fry for a few more minutes.

Soak the saffron strands in warm milk. Rub the strands in milk to dissolve them completely. Keep aside for 5 minutes. Add rose essence and kewra water and set aside for another 15 minutes.

Grease the bottom of a large handi with ghee.

Layer the bottom with bay leaves. This helps infuse a lovely fragrance into the biryani and prevents the bottom layer from burning.

Now, to begin layering, add a layer of cooked rice, cooked meat pieces, 1 or 2 potatoes, and an egg (or halved egg pieces).

Sprinkle the saffron-infused milk, biryani masala, and melted ghee over each layer.

Repeat this process until all ingredients are used.

Cover the handi with a lid and seal the edges completely with kneaded dough. Place something heavy on top of the lid (such as a sil batta) before starting the dum cooking.

Cook on medium-low heat for 40 minutes.

After switching off the flame, let the biryani rest for 10 minutes before opening the lid.

Serving suggestion: Serve immediately with raita.

Mutton Dak Bungalow
by Reetika Mitra, West Bengal

This dish carries a colonial heritage, tracing its roots in the days of the East India Company, when Dak Bungalows were found across India. Several dishes emerged during this period, and some have remained popular to this day.

Mutton Dak Bungalow is one such recipe, rich in history. Interestingly, the recipe for this dish varies depending on the geographical location of the Dak Bungalows, influencing the choice of spices and ingredients. In this version, I've blended the finest elements from different variations of this recipe. I have incorporated potatoes and eggs, which are common ingredients in most Dak Bungalow recipes. While this dish traditionally uses mutton, it can easily be substituted with chicken using the same method.

For the mutton version, it's advisable to prepare the dish a day in advance to allow the meat to tenderize and the flavours to deepen. Although the recipe may seem a bit labour-intensive, the results are well worth the effort!

MUTTON DAK BUNGALOW
(Slow-cooked Mutton Curry)

REETIKA MITRA

WEST BENGAL

SERVES: 5

PREPARATION TIME: 2–4 HOURS

COOK TIME: 60 MINUTES

INGREDIENTS

Mutton	1 kg, with bone
Mustard oil	4 tbsp
Desi ghee	2 tbsp
Bay leaves	2
Onions	2, large, finely chopped
Tomatoes	2, medium-sized, diced into quarters
Green chillies	1–2, finely chopped or to taste
Turmeric powder	½ tsp
Kashmiri red chilli powder	1 tsp
Onion	1, large, cut into quarters
Garlic	2 tbsp, finely chopped
Ginger	2 tbsp, finely chopped
Sugar	1 tsp, heaped
Boiled eggs	6
Potatoes (optional)	5–6, halved
Hot water	250 ml
Salt	to taste

FOR THE MARINADE:

Curd	3 tbsp
Garlic paste	1 tbsp
Ginger paste	1 tbsp
Turmeric	½ tsp
Cumin powder	½ tsp
Coriander powder	½ tsp
Red chilli powder	½ tsp

Lemon juice	1 tbsp
Mustard oil	2 tbsp
Salt	1 tsp

DRY ROAST AND GRINDING:

Green cardamom	4–5
Cinnamon stick	1 inch
Cloves	4
Dry red chillies	2–3 or to taste
Coriander seeds	½ tsp
Cumin seeds	½ tsp
Black peppercorns	¼ tsp
Nutmeg powder	¼ tsp
Mace powder	¼ tsp

METHOD

Wash and pat dry the mutton pieces. In a bowl, mix all the ingredients for the marinade and coat the mutton well. Seal it with a cling film and refrigerate for 2 to 4 hours.

Heat a griddle or tawa over medium-low flame. Dry roast all the ingredients listed under 'Dry roast and grinding' until they release a fragrant aroma and turn lightly toasted. Be careful not to over-roast or burn the spices. Turn off the flame and let them cool at room temperature.

Once cooled, transfer the roasted spices to a grinder. Grind them into a fine powder. Add chopped garlic, chopped ginger, 1 cut onion to the grinder and blend everything into a smooth paste, along with the roasted spice powder. Keep them ready to be used during cooking.

Peel the boiled eggs and prick the skin with a toothpick. Marinate them with a pinch of turmeric powder and salt. If using potatoes, peel and marinate them in the same way.

Heat 2–3 tablespoons of oil in a deep-bottomed pan and

shallow fry the marinated eggs until light golden brown. Remove and set aside on paper towels. Next, shallow fry the marinated potatoes in the same oil until they turn golden brown. Drain them similarly. Set them aside as well.

In the same pan, heat the remaining oil and ghee. When hot, temper with bay leaves, then add the two chopped onions and green chillies. Stir for a bit, then add the diced tomatoes, turmeric powder, Kashmiri red chilli powder, salt, and sugar.

Stir regularly, cooking for 3–4 minutes until the oil is released, and the raw masalas are cooked. Add the marinated mutton to the pan and mix well. Stir and cook for another 10 minutes over medium heat.

Now, add the dry roasted and ground masala paste mix to the mutton. Mix thoroughly and cook for 5–7 minutes over medium flame, stirring regularly.

Add 250 ml of hot water, cover, and cook over medium-low flame for 50 minutes to 1 hour, or till the mutton is 80 per cent tender and soft. Remember to stir at regular intervals.

At this stage, add the shallow-fried eggs and potatoes to the mutton. Stir frequently and cook for another 5–10 minutes over medium heat until the meat is fully cooked and the potatoes are tender.

Lastly, add 1 teaspoon of ghee, mix well, and switch off the flame.

Garnish with chopped coriander leaves and green chillies.

Serving suggestion: Serve hot with plain rice, naan, rotis, parathas, or pooris.

Note: For best results, marinate overnight, but remember to bring the mutton to room temperature for about an hour before cooking.

If you have shortage of time, there is another method to

make the delicious Mutton Dak Bungalow.

ALTERNATIVE METHOD

After adding the roasted and ground masala paste and 250 ml of hot water, transfer the mutton to a pressure cooker.

Cook on high flame until the first whistle. Lower the flame and continue cooking for another 15 minutes.

Now, take off the lid and add the shallow-fried eggs and potatoes to the mutton.

Stir frequently over medium heat and cook for another 3–4 minutes without closing the lid. The mutton can also be transferred to a deep-bottomed pan if it helps with stirring.

Add some more water if necessary, depending on your desired gravy thickness.

Cook for about 8 to 10 minutes until the gravy thickens, and adjust seasoning to taste. Lastly, add 1 teaspoon of ghee, mix well and garnish with coriander leaves and green chillies.

Mutton Masala
by Jennifer Lobo, Karnataka

My mother-in-law, Juliana Lobo, was blessed with incredible culinary skills that she had inherited from her mother. She was the best cook in the family, and everyone who had the pleasure of tasting them always adored the dishes she prepared. She was generous in sharing her recipes, passing down a few of her tips and secrets to me, which she had learned from her maternal lineage.

In Mangalore, almost every gravy incorporates coconut—whether grated, ground into masala, or in the form of coconut milk—an obvious choice since coconut is abundant and easily available in the region. The rich, coconut-based gravies complement the local red rice beautifully, creating a harmonious balance of flavours.

For me, grating and grinding coconut had always been a tedious task. So, during one of our conversations, I asked her if there was any dish that didn't require coconut but still retained the essence of our native flavours. To my surprise, she introduced me to this particular recipe, which does not have coconut in any form. It's simple, easy to make, and still brings out the authentic flavours of our native cuisine.

MUTTON MASALA
(Flavourful Mutton Curry)

JENNIFER LOBO | KARNATAKA
SERVES: 5–6 | PREPARATION TIME: 15 MINUTES
COOK TIME: 30 MINUTES

INGREDIENTS

Mutton	1 kg, medium-sized pieces
Desi ghee	2–3 tbsp
Onions	5, large, finely sliced
Tomatoes	2, finely chopped
Ginger	1 inch, grated
Garlic	½ pod, finely chopped
Cloves	2–3
Cinnamon	½ inch stick
Kashmiri red chillies	4–6
Coriander seeds	1 tbsp
Cumin seeds	2 tbsp
Black peppercorns	6–8
Turmeric powder	1 tsp
Tamarind	10 gms (seedless)
Salt	to taste
Water	250 ml (approx.)
Coriander leaves	chopped, to garnish

METHOD

In a large pan, heat ghee over medium heat. Add the finely sliced onions and cook for five minutes on low flame, stirring occasionally until the onions turn light brown.

Add the chopped garlic, grated ginger, cinnamon stick, and chopped tomatoes in the pan.

Sauté until the tomatoes turn slightly tender. If the mixture begins to dry out or stick to the bottom of the pan, add a tablespoon of water.

Add the mutton pieces to the pan and cook for another 5–10 minutes.

Meanwhile, grind the Kashmiri red chillies, coriander seeds, cumin seeds, cloves, black peppercorns, turmeric powder, and tamarind into a smooth paste.

Pour this paste over the mutton and mix well to coat it thoroughly. Season with salt, as per taste. Cover the pan with a lid that has a cavity on top for water. Fill the lid with water and let the mutton cook on low flame.

As the water in the lid begins to steam, replace it with fresh cool water. Repeat this process until the mutton is fully cooked.

Add warm water to the pan to adjust the gravy to your desired consistency.

Once the mutton is cooked, garnish the dish with freshly chopped coriander leaves.

Serving suggestion: Serve hot with naan, kulcha, roti, Mangalorean sannas (soft fluffy rice cakes/idlis), pao, or steamed rice.

Kerala Mutton Ishtew
by Rekha Abraham Verghese, Kerala

I first learned this delectable dish from my sister-in-law during my first visit to Kerala. As a North Indian, I had no prior knowledge of it, but I instantly fell in love the moment I tried it. Mutton Stew, or 'Ishtew', is a traditional dish often made by Syrian Christians in Kerala.

It took me a while to fully grasp the complex flavours, but today, I'm proud to say that I've perfected my version of this dish. It has become my signature recipe.

KERALA MUTTON ISHTEW
(Kerala-style Mutton Stew)

REKHA ABRAHAM VERGHESE — KERALA

SERVES: 5 — PREPARATION TIME: 30 MINUTES

COOK TIME: 45 MINUTES

INGREDIENTS

FOR THE MUTTON:

Mutton raan pieces	1 kg
Ginger-garlic paste	2 tbsp
Curry leaves	1 sprig

Salt	1 tsp or to taste
Pepper powder	1 tsp
Water	500 ml
Potatoes	2, medium-sized, cut into halves

FOR THE CURRY:

Coconut oil	3 tbsp
Vegetable oil	1 tbsp
Fennel seeds	2 tsp
Star anise	3
Cinnamon sticks	3
Green cardamom	4
Cloves	4
Ginger-garlic	3 tbsp, juliennes
Green chillies	3, slit longitudinally
Curry leaves	3 sprigs
Onions	3, medium-sized, finely sliced
Salt	1 tsp or to taste
Carrots	2, cut into cubes
Potatoes	2, medium-sized, cut into cubes
Garam masala	3 tsp
Water	150 ml
Cashews	30 gms, made into paste
Coconut milk	250 ml, thick consistency (2 coconuts freshly grated, squeezed, and strained by adding 200 ml of lukewarm water to make 250 ml thick consistency coconut milk)
Pepper	2 tsp

METHOD

Cover the mutton with ginger-garlic paste, curry leaves, salt, and pepper powder. Let it marinate for 15 minutes.

In a pressure cooker, add the marinated mutton with 500 ml of water and potatoes cut into halves.

Cook for 3 whistles or till the mutton is fully cooked and tender. Leave it aside.

In a large-sized pot or kadhai, heat 2 tablespoons of coconut oil and 1 tablespoon of vegetable oil. Once hot, add all the whole spices and sauté for about 30 seconds. Then, add the juliennes of ginger-garlic, slit green chillies, 2 sprigs of curry leaves, and sauté for another minute.

Now, add the finely sliced onions and 1 teaspoon of salt. Sauté until the onions become translucent.

Add the diced carrots and potatoes, mix well, and cook for 4 minutes.

Add 2 teaspoons of garam masala powder and sauté everything well.

Pour in 150 ml of warm water, cover the pan with a lid, and let the vegetables cook.

Now, add the boiled mutton with the potatoes to the kadhai and mix everything. Continue to cook for another 5 minutes over medium flame.

Then, add the cashew paste and cook for 2 minutes.

Add the fresh coconut milk, mix well, and cook for another 2 minutes. Turn off the heat.

Add 2 teaspoons of black pepper powder, the remaining garam masala powder, and mix well.

Garnish with curry leaves and 1 tablespoon of coconut oil (optional). Cover the kadhai and let it rest for 15 minutes.

Serving suggestion: Serve hot with steamed rice or appams.

Gosht ke Pasande

by Anamika Bajpai, Awadh

I come from a vegetarian Lucknowi Brahmin household, yet my siblings and I have always been very fond of non-vegetarian food, especially mutton. During the Eid celebrations at our parents' friends' home, we would relish the lavish spread of celebratory dishes like pasande, qorma, salan, biryani, mussallam, and many more. These feasts, where the food was undoubtedly the most important part of the occasion, were always the ones we eagerly anticipated.

I distinctly remember the tantalizing aromas of typical Awadhi food, infused with kewra and saffron, greeting us as soon as we stepped into the old-fashioned verandas of their kothi. A seasoned cook, from a well-known family with great culinary fame in the city, once told me, 'Baaki sab seekh sakte hain, par pasande toh kala hai, ye seekhi nahi jaati, it's only inherited.' (One can learn to cook anything except pasande—cooking pasande is an art, it can only be inherited.) Unfortunately, I had no one to inherit it from.

Undeterred, I did my research—reading, watching videos, and grasping the nuances of the dish—and created my own recipe. When that same cook tasted my version, they asked me which bawarchi had prepared it. They couldn't believe that I had made it. But that was never my aim—to prove it to others. My goal was always to learn for myself, to quench my own thirst for knowledge.

Today, I take pride in preparing some of the most amazing Gosht ke Pasande. I truly hope that one day, the children in my family will inherit it from me, making it a cherished heirloom to pass down through generations.

GOSHT KE PASANDE
(Marinated Lamb in Spiced Gravy)

ANAMIKA BAJPAI — AWADH

SERVES: 4–5 — PREPARATION TIME: 1 HOUR

COOK TIME: 1 HOUR 30 MINUTES

INGREDIENTS

Mutton pasande	500 gms

FOR THE MARINADE:

Curd	250 gms, fresh, non-sour
Ginger paste	2 tbsp
Garlic paste	1 tbsp
Salt	½ tbsp
Yellow chilli powder	½ tbsp
Mace	1 tsp
Green cardamom powder	1 tsp

FOR TEMPERING:

Desi ghee	100 ml
Green cardamom	2
Cloves	4
Black peppercorns	6
Royal or black cumin seeds	½ tsp
Cinnamon	2-inch piece
Black cardamom	1

FOR THE GRAVY:

Desiccated coconut	2 tbsp
Almonds	10, whole, soaked and peeled
Cashews	5, whole, soaked
Melon seeds	2 tbsp
Birista (golden fried onions)	2 tbsp
Milk	150 ml
Hot water	300 ml

FOR THE INFUSION:

Kewra	1 tsp
Meetha ittar	2–3 drops
Mace	½ tsp
Green cardamom powder	½ tsp
Homemade garam masala powder	½ tsp
Saffron	Few strands, lightly crushed and soaked in 1 tbsp water

FOR GARNISHING:

Chaandi ki warq (edible microthin silver sheets)	3–4 strips
Almonds	1 tbsp, slivered
Ginger	1 tbsp, julienned

METHOD

Mix all the ingredients for the marinade and coat the mutton pasande thoroughly. Keep aside for 45 minutes to marinate.

Grind all the ingredients listed for the gravy into a fine paste and set it aside.

Heat ghee in a copper lagan (if available) or in a flat-bottomed aluminium handi to prepare the tempering. On the lowest flame, sauté the whole spices for tempering for about 30 seconds, allowing the ghee to get infused with their flavours.

Slowly add the marinated pasande to the lagan, and sauté on low-medium flame.

Cook for about 20 minutes, and then add a little hot water. Cover and cook on a low flame for another 30 minutes, stirring at regular intervals.

Gradually add the prepared gravy paste, coating the pasande fillets well.

Sauté the mixture, then add about 100 ml of warm water. Be careful since the gravy will be thick and may splutter.

Cover the pan and cook for 15 minutes more on low flame, or until the ghee separates and the fillets are completely cooked. Check for salt and add as needed.

Now, add in all the ingredients listed under infusion. Give it a last light stir. Switch off the flame.

Allow it to rest for 30 minutes.

Garnish with chaandi ki warq, almond slivers, and ginger juliennes, and serve hot.

Hare Masale ki Chaap

by Shibani Chand Sethi, Uttar Pradesh

In the heart of Bangalore stood Nanaji's bustling home, where hospitality flowed as freely as the tea. As a respected police officer, Nanaji's door was always open to friends, family, and colleagues, who would often drop by unannounced. Nanima, his wife, was the queen of the kitchen, adept at creating quick, delicious meals to feed the steady stream of guests.

One day, with a sudden influx of visitors and only mutton in the pantry, Nanima improvised. She blended fresh green herbs—coriander, mint, and chillies—with spices, marinated the mutton chops, and cooked them to perfection. The result was Hare Masale ki Chaap, a dish bursting with tangy, spicy, and aromatic flavours.

The guests were captivated by the unique taste, and the recipe quickly became a favourite. As more people tasted the dish, its fame grew. Nanima's Hare Masale ki Chaap became a signature dish of the family, passed down through generations, each adding their own touch but always keeping the essence of her original creation.

Today, the Hare Masale ki Chaap is more than just a recipe; it is a treasured family tradition, a reminder of the warmth, love, and quick thinking that defined Nanima's kitchen and made every meal an event to remember.

HARE MASALE KI CHAAP
(Mutton Chaap with Green Spice Blend)

SHIBANI CHAND SETHI | UTTAR PRADESH

SERVES: 4–6 | PREPARATION TIME: 20–30 MINUTES

COOK TIME: 30–40 MINUTES

INGREDIENTS

Double mutton chops	1 kg
Desi ghee	2 tbsp
Turmeric powder	1 tsp
Salt	to taste
Onion	1, large, thinly sliced, to garnish

FOR THE MASALA:

Onions	4, large, thickly sliced
Coriander leaves	250 gms
Mint leaves	50 gms
Coriander powder	2 tsp, heaped
Black peppercorns	2 tsp, heaped
Fennel seeds	1 tsp, heaped
Garlic	2 full cloves, peeled
Green chillies	20, small
Ginger	4, small
Cinnamon	3–4, small

METHOD

Hit the mutton chops with a mallet to flatten them out.

Grind all the ingredients for the masala in a mixer with a little water to make a fine paste.

Lay out the chops in a flat-bottomed pan or degchi on medium-low flame and add just enough water to cover them.

Add 1 teaspoon of turmeric powder and salt to taste.

When the chops are almost cooked, add the ground masala and cook on high flame, keeping the pan covered.

Cook for 30 minutes, stirring occasionally to prevent burning.

In a separate kadhai, heat 2 tablespoons of ghee and add the cooked chops. Mix well and let it cook for another 4–5 minutes.

Serving suggestion: Garnish with thinly sliced, round onions.

Note: For a tangier flavour, add 1 tablespoon of lemon juice to the chaap.

Seafood

Bhapa Ilish

by Ruma Bhattacharjee, West Bengal

As a young bride, I was enchanted by the grandeur of my father-in-law's market excursions.

Like a true Bengali babu, he would return home with a bountiful selection of fresh vegetables and fish, all carried by a loyal porter. But the majestic Ilish always received the most attention. When he brought home this silver beauty, he would cradle it like a trophy, refusing to let anyone else touch it. My mother-in-law would then take on the daunting task of cutting the Ilish, something that required both precision and patience. But she didn't mind, for she knew it was her husband's one true passion.

The first day of Ilish was always a celebration—whether steamed to perfection in a fragrant bhapa, fried to a golden crisp, or cooked in a zesty tel jhol. The pièce de résistance? The residual oil, infused with the essence of Ilish, served with steamed rice and fried green chillies. We called it Ilish Machbhaja Tel, a delicacy that still makes Bengali hearts skip a beat. But the true star was always the Bhapa Ilish, a dish fit for the gods. In those moments, I knew I was part of something special—a family bound by love, tradition, and the unbridled joy of savouring life's simple pleasures.

BHAPA ILISH
(Steamed Hilsa Fish in Mustard Sauce)

RUMA BHATTACHARJEE — WEST BENGAL

SERVES: 3–4 — PREPARATION TIME: 15 MINUTES

COOK TIME: 15 MINUTES

INGREDIENTS

Ilish fish	500 gms, cut into 5–6 pieces
Green chillies	8–10, slit longitudinally
Black mustard seeds	3 tbsp
Yellow mustard seeds	3 tbsp
Turmeric powder	½ tbsp
Salt	1 tbsp
Mustard oil	50 ml
Water	300 ml (approx.)

METHOD

Wash the Ilish pieces thoroughly and keep them aside.

Rinse both the black and yellow mustard seeds and grind them into a smooth paste with 5 green chillies, 2 tablespoons of water, and half a tablespoon of salt.

Add turmeric powder, 4 tablespoons of water, 3–4 tablespoons of mustard oil, and the remaining salt to the mustard paste. Mix well to form a paste-like marinade.

Marinate the Ilish pieces with this paste, ensuring they are evenly coated.

Put a broad pan or skillet on medium flame and fill it with 200 ml of water.

Now, place the marinated fish pieces inside a steel tiffin box or a steel pot with a lid. Pour the leftover marinade and mustard oil over the fish pieces.

Place the green chillies on top of the fish. Close the box/

pot and place it inside the hot water in the skillet. Cover the skillet with a lid to trap the steam, and allow the fish to cook for 10–12 minutes.

Turn off the flame and let it sit, covered, for another 4–5 minutes.

Carefully remove the tiffin box/pot from the skillet. Open the lid cautiously to avoid any escaping residual steam.

Serving suggestion: Serve the Bhapa Ilish with steamed rice for a truly divine experience!

Chingrir Chodchodi

by Deepa Dutta Chaudhuri, West Bengal

This dish, Chingrir Chodchodi, has deep roots in my father's side of the family. My paternal grandmother used to prepare it with great care in our Shillong home, ensuring that all the vegetables—from jhinge (sponge gourd) and padwal to daanta (full-grown amaranth stems)—were fresh. Cooked in strong mustard oil, it was a hit in the house. On days when Chingrir Chodchodi was on the menu, nothing else was needed with rice. Over the years, my mother learned the recipe from her and, in time, mastered it.

It's important to note here that my maiden home is unequivocally Bangal—Bengalis with roots in what is now Bangladesh. Both sets of my grandparents moved from Dhaka to West Bengal during the Partition of India in 1947.

Fast forward to 2004, and I got married and joined the Ghoti (Bengalis originally from West Bengal) household of the Chaudhuris. They love their prawns and treat them like royalty, making rich dishes like Malai Curry or Bhapa Chingri. My husband couldn't fathom the idea of mixing prawns with vegetables! 'Are you nuts? Lowly vegetables with the royal prawns?' he'd ask indignantly. And so, my love affair with my childhood favourite Chingrir Chodchodi came to an abrupt end. After marriage, with my limited cooking skills, I never bothered to make it just for myself.

Things changed, however, when I was pregnant with my daughter. I couldn't cook fish during my first trimester—the smell was revolting to me. That's when Maa made Chingrir Chodchodi for me and requested my husband to try just a spoonful. After that blessed spoonful, we had a minor convert—Ghoti to Bangal. Since then, the dish has become so popular in our home that whenever my husband spots small prawns at the fish market, he immediately thinks of Chingrir Chodchodi and buys all the necessary vegetables. These days, we make it whenever the amaranths in my garden are ready to be used in the chodchodi.

CHINGRIR CHODCHODI
(Prawn Stir-Fry with Vegetables)

DEEPA DUTTA CHAUDHURI — WEST BENGAL

SERVES: 4 — PREPARATION TIME: 30–45 MINUTES

COOK TIME: 20–30 MINUTES

INGREDIENTS

Prawns	500 gms, small-sized, de-veined with heads
Potatoes	2–3
Jhinge (sponge gourd)	2–3
Carrots	2–3
Padwal (snake gourd)	2–3
Daanta (amaranth)	2–3
Long brinjals	2–3
Beans	100 gms
Green chillies	7–8, slit longitudinally
Bay leaves	2
Cumin seeds	½ tsp
Turmeric powder	1 tsp

Mustard oil	5 tbsp
Salt	to taste
Sugar	to taste

METHOD

In a large kadhai, heat 1 tablespoon of mustard oil. Once hot, add the bay leaves. Next, add cumin seeds, and as soon as they splutter, add the green chillies. Toss in the prawns, sauté lightly until they turn a bit pink, and keep aside.

Heat another tablespoon of mustard oil in the kadhai. Sauté the potatoes, carrots, padwal, and daanta on high flame, one after the other. Set them aside once they become slightly glossy.

Next, adding oil as required, sauté the brinjals, beans, and sponge gourd separately.

Now add all the vegetables and prawns to the kadhai. Sprinkle salt and turmeric powder over the mixture and stir gently to coat everything with the seasoning.

Lower the flame, cover the kadhai with a lid, and let the lot cook in its own juices until everything is well cooked. Do not add water—this dish should remain dry, and the vegetables should retain some bite.

If any excess water remains, stir on high heat to evaporate it.

Add a pinch of sugar. Stir well and switch off the stove. Now, drizzle in some raw mustard oil, give it a final stir, and cover to let the aroma infuse.

Serving suggestion: Serve hot and savour with steamed rice.

Note: The key to a good chodchodi lies in cutting the vegetables uniformly, about one-and-a-half-inch cubes, to ensure proper cooking and texture. Keep the dish simple with just turmeric powder and salt, and no other spices, and let the flavours of prawns and veggies shine.

Kottayam Fish Curry
by Divya Sreeji, Kerala

This was the first dish my amma, mother-in-law, taught me. Since then, it has been our family favourite for the last twenty-four years. Every time I make it, it brings back memories of our lives in England and Holland, as I reminisce about how I've refined it over the years with my own little touches. The moment when Amma told me that my version of the dish was even better than her original will forever remain close to my heart. Now that she's no longer with us, this dish holds an even more special place in our family. It preserves her memory and our bond.

KOTTAYAM FISH CURRY
(Kerala-style Fish Curry)

DIVYA SREEJI	KERALA
SERVES: 3–4	PREPARATION TIME: 40 MINUTES
	COOK TIME: 25 MINUTES

INGREDIENTS

Seer fish (king fish or surmai)	500 gms, cut into medium-sized pieces
Onions	2, medium-sized, finely chopped
Garlic	7–8 cloves, crushed

Ginger	a small piece, crushed
Curry leaves	1 sprig
Dry red chillies	4
Coriander powder	1 tbsp
Kashmiri red chilli powder	3 tbsp
Turmeric powder	1 tsp
Asafoetida	a pinch
Salt	to taste
Mustard seeds	1 tsp
Coconut oil	4 tbsp
Tomato paste	2 tbsp
Tomato	1, small-sized, finely chopped
Kodampuli (tamarind)	3 pieces
Water	15 tbsp

METHOD

Soak 3 pieces of kodampuli in approximately 15 tablespoons of water for 30 minutes. Set them aside.

In a traditional clay pan, heat some oil and add mustard seeds. Let them splutter.

Add crushed ginger, garlic, onions, and dry red chillies. Sauté until golden brown.

Now, add Kashmiri red chilli powder, turmeric powder, and coriander powder, along with asafoetida and salt to taste.

Stir in tomatoes, tomato paste, half of the curry leaves, and soaked tamarind with water. Mix well and cover the pan with a lid. Let it cook for 10 minutes.

Remove the lid, stir well, and gently add the fish pieces. Cover again and cook for 15 minutes till the fish is fully cooked and the oil separates.

To garnish, add the remaining curry leaves.

Serving suggestion: Serve hot with steamed rice.

Mangalorean Prawn Ghassi

by Vaishali Kolpe Sabherwal, Karnataka

Saraswat or Konkani cuisine from Mangalore is renowned for its rich, coconut-infused gravies and spicy curries. The seafood preparations are possibly some of the most delicious dishes ever. As a little girl, I vividly remember my mother preparing mouth-watering Prawn or 'sungta' Ghassi for us—a dish we loved. It was a cherished ritual in our home—my mother would personally handpick the freshest prawns from the local 'macchiwali', who arrived at our doorstep on weekends with the morning catch from the Arabian Sea.

Curious and eager, I would sit beside the macchiwali's cane basket, wide-eyed in amazement at the variety of seafood she carried—gleaming fish, mussels, and even crabs. I watched intently as my mother, with her discerning eye, carefully selected the best prawns and handed them over to be cleaned and deveined.

I would then excitedly follow my mother to the kitchen as she slow-roasted a handful of aromatic spices in a pan, filling the air with a heady scent that seemed to wrap itself around our home. But nothing compared to the magic of those prawns simmering in the curry over a gentle flame, their flavours blending into an ambrosial delight!

I can still recall the intoxicating fragrance of those magical spices wafting through the entire house and the eager anticipation on my brother's face and mine as we sat at the table, awaiting the delicious meal!

MANGALOREAN PRAWN GHASSI
(Spicy Coconut Prawn Curry)

VAISHALI KOLPE SABHERWAL — KARNATAKA (KONKAN)

SERVES: 4–5 — PREPARATION TIME: 15 MINUTES

COOK TIME: 25 MINUTES

INGREDIENTS

Prawns	500 gms, cleaned and deveined
Coconut	100 gms, grated
Coriander seeds	2 tbsp
Cumin seeds	1 tsp
Black peppercorns	1 tsp
Fenugreek seeds	½ tsp
Turmeric powder	½ tsp
Red chilli powder	1 tbsp
Onion	1, medium-sized, finely chopped
Green chillies	2–3, slit longitudinally
Tamarind pulp	1 tbsp
Coconut oil	2–3 tbsp
Curry leaves	1 sprig
Salt	to taste
Water	400 ml

METHOD

In a pan, dry roast the coriander seeds, cumin seeds, black peppercorns, and fenugreek seeds until fragrant. Let them cool.

Grind the roasted spices with grated coconut, turmeric powder, and red chilli powder to a smooth paste, adding a little water if needed.

Now, heat coconut oil in a large pan over medium flame. Add the finely chopped onions and sauté until golden brown.

Add the slit green chillies and curry leaves and sauté for another minute.

Then, add the ground masala paste to the pan. Cook, stirring continuously, until the oil begins to separate from the masala.

Add the prawns to the pan and mix them thoroughly with the masala paste.

Add tamarind pulp and salt to taste.

Pour in approximately 400 ml of water to achieve a gravy-like consistency.

Bring the curry to a boil, then reduce the heat and let it simmer for 10–15 minutes, allowing the prawns to cook and the flavours to meld.

Serving suggestion: This flavourful and aromatic coastal dish is best served hot with fluffy, steamed rice or neer dosa!

Malwani Crab Curry
by Kavita Bagga, Maharashtra

Though my roots are in Jammu and Kashmir and Punjab, I have spent a considerable part of my life in Maharashtra, especially between Mumbai and Goa. It was here that my love affair with seafood began, and I learned many local dishes from the humble homes of my domestic staff. The ocean feeds the world, and living by the coast offers a profound understanding of its role in sustaining life. I have often sat by the sea, watching the hopeful fishermen set out at sunrise with their nets and return joyously with the fresh catch of the day. Every bountiful haul makes up for those less fortunate days when the nets return empty.

My favourite sight is the little kids who run up to these boats as they wash ashore, eager to pick up any fish or shrimp that may slip through the nets—these often become their next meal. Among all the dishes I've embraced, Malwani Crab Curry holds a special place in my heart. It has become a family favourite, and I believe it has also earned me culinary acclaim among friends!

MALWANI CRAB CURRY
(Crab Curry with Coconut and Spice Blend)

KAVITA BAGGA — MAHARASHTRA

SERVES: 5–6 — PREPARATION TIME: 15 MINUTES

COOK TIME: 60 MINUTES

INGREDIENTS

Crabs	8, small, cleaned and cut into pieces

FOR THE PASTE:

Byadagi red chillies	4
Red chilli powder	1 tsp
Coriander seeds	2 tsp
Fennel seeds	1½ tsp
Fenugreek seeds	¼ tsp
Cumin seeds	1 tsp
Black peppercorns	⅓ tsp
Green cardamom	2–3
Cinnamon	1-inch piece
Fresh coconut	200 gms, grated

FOR THE CURRY:

Onions	2, large, chopped
Ginger	½ tbsp, grated
Garlic	½ tbsp, chopped and smashed
Coconut milk	400 ml
Curry leaves	2–3 sprigs
Tomatoes	2, medium-sized, finely chopped
Kokum	3–4 pieces, soaked in warm water
Coconut oil	2–3 tbsp
Coriander leaves	2 tbsp, finely chopped, to garnish
Salt	to taste

METHOD

Dry roast all the spices for the paste until aromatic. Ensure that the spices don't burn. Then, grind them with the grated coconut to make a coarse paste and keep aside.

Heat coconut oil in a kadhai or deep wok. Add the chopped onions and sauté until tender.

Add the curry leaves, ginger, and garlic. Sauté until the mixture turns golden brown.

Now, add the tomatoes and dry masala paste made earlier. Cook until the oil separates from the mixture.

Add salt and a little coconut milk. Cook until well combined.

Once the curry is well cooked, add the rest of the coconut milk and let it come to a boil. The quantity of coconut milk can be adjusted as per the desired curry consistency.

Then, add the crabs and soaked kokum pieces to the curry.

Cover and cook for about 15 minutes, or till the crabs are fully cooked and the shells turn orange.

Garnish with freshly chopped coriander.

Serving suggestion: Serve hot with white or rosematta rice.

Pickles and Chutneys

Khajoor Chutney

by Arvinder Kaur Chawla, New Delhi

The origin of this recipe dates back to the late 1960s. One of my paternal aunts was very weak during her first pregnancy, with severely low haemoglobin levels. The doctors advised her to consume iron-rich foods, like dates, but she had a strong aversion to them and would often vomit when trying to eat them. A neighbour suggested she suck on ginger to ease her nausea, and it worked. Inspired by this, her younger sister came up with the idea of combining dates and ginger. The challenge, however, was to make this combination both healthy and tasty. Another aunt recommended creating a chutney using these two primary ingredients, along with nutritious almonds, raisins, and an assortment of other nuts. This is how the Khajoor Chutney was first made in my family—a recipe lovingly created to support my aunt and one that has since been cherished and enjoyed across generations.

KHAJOOR CHUTNEY
(Date Chutney)

ARVINDER KAUR CHAWLA NEW DELHI

MAKES: 350 GMS CHUTNEY PREPARATION TIME: 1 HOUR (FOR SOAKING)

COOK TIME: 30 MINUTES

INGREDIENTS

Khajoor (dates)	200 gms, deseeded
Almonds	4 tbsp, chopped lengthwise
Raisins, apricots, figs, walnuts (optional)	5 tbsp combined, chopped
White vinegar	100 ml
Ginger	200 gms, peeled and julienned
Olive oil	3 tbsp
Salt	1 tsp
Black salt	½ tsp
Black pepper powder	to taste
Cumin powder	to taste, roasted
Water	200 ml (approx.)

METHOD

Take the dates and deseed them. In a pan, put these deseeded and cleaned dates, then cover them with water. Let them soak for an hour.

Bring the mixture to a boil for 5 minutes or until the dates soften. Strain the water from the softened dates and set aside.

Take a fresh pan and heat 3 tbsp of olive oil (or any bland oil). Add the ginger juliennes and sauté for 2–3 minutes. Next, add the almonds and sauté for another minute. Then, add the vinegar, softened dates, raisins, and the other dry fruits being used.

Let the concoction come together and cook for a while. If it becomes too thick or lumpy, gradually add the reserved date water to adjust the consistency.

Season it with salt, pepper, and cumin powder. Continue to cook till you get the desired chutney consistency and glaze. Taste and adjust the seasoning as needed.

Let it cool and your Khajoor Chutney is ready.

Once cooled, store the chutney in a sterilized, airtight glass jar.

Serving suggestions: The chutney can be relished with parathas or any kind of bread, without any guilt of consuming sugar.

Note: Ginger imparts a tart taste to the chutney, vinegar balances the sourness, and raisins and dates provide sweetness.

Khatta Masaledar Nimbu ka Achaar

by Monalika Sabharwal, Rajasthan

My mom was incredibly fortunate to inherit a recipe of an oil-free whole lemon pickle, crafted with a blend of spices and special techniques from her father-in-law. He, in turn, had received it from the royal head chef of the king of Bharatpur, Rajasthan.

This recipe holds a special place in my heart. I remember my grandfather, grandmother, and mom preparing this pickle together for the entire family and extended relatives. Every year, everyone eagerly anticipated the chance to savour these exquisite whole lemons!

I feel truly blessed to have received this recipe a few years ago and to be able to carry on the tradition with some measure of success and a lot of pride!

KHATTA MASALEDAR NIMBU KA ACHAAR
(Tangy and Spicy Lemon Pickle)

MONALIKA SABHARWAL RAJASTHAN

MAKES: 500 GMS PREPARATION TIME: 30 MINUTES

COOK TIME: 3–4 DAYS

INGREDIENTS

Lemons	10, large, juicy

DRY SPICES:

Salt	3 tbsp
Black salt	1 tbsp
Red chilli powder	1 tbsp
Fennel seeds	1½ tbsp, coarsely ground
Fenugreek seeds	1 tbsp
Carom seeds	1 tsp
Turmeric powder	1 tsp
Asafoetida	½ tsp

METHOD

Wash and clean the lemons thoroughly. Ensure they are completely dry by wiping them with a clean cloth.

In a bowl, combine all the dry spices like red chilli powder, turmeric powder, fenugreek seeds, carom seeds, coarsely ground fennel seeds, and asafoetida.

Slit each lemon into four equal parts, ensuring the lemon stays joint at one end.

Squeeze the lemons to get about half the juice out, but leave some juice in the lemons. This will make the achaar taste better. Use a sieve to strain the juice and take out any seeds.

Generously fill the dry spice mixture into the slits in the

lemons.

Clean a glass jar using a dry cloth. Sprinkle some of the dry spice mixture inside it.

Place the spice-filled lemons in the jar and pour the strained lemon juice on top of the lemons, covering them.

Sprinkle some more of the dry spice mix on top of the lemons in the jar.

Close the lid of the jar tightly and shake it gently.

Store the jar in a cool, dry place for 3–4 days, avoiding direct sunlight. The lemon pickle is ready to be enjoyed.

Serving suggestion: This delicious lemon pickle can be enjoyed with warm parathas, chapatis, or rice, along with any curry or vegetables.

Note: The lemons should be large and juicy.

All utensils used in the preparation must be clean and completely dry, with no moisture present in them.

Puli Inji
by Binu Menon, Kerala

Puli Inji, a traditional Kerala dish, holds a cherished place in our family's culinary heritage, especially during Onam celebrations. This sweet and sour ginger pickle is not just a condiment; it's a symbol of love, tradition, and unity. My grandmother, or Ammumma, was renowned for her Puli Inji recipe, passed down through generations of our family.

Every year, as Onam approached, Ammumma would meticulously prepare the ingredients, her hands guided by years of experience. The preparation of Puli Inji was a family affair, with each member playing an important role. The task of finely chopping ginger in the traditional wooden utensil called paaththi was usually entrusted to the men of the household. The rhythmic sound of chopping and the sweet, tangy aroma of Puli Inji would fill our home, signalling the start of the festivities.

As children, we would gather around Ammumma, watching in awe as she expertly balanced the flavours. While helping her prepare the pickle, she would share stories of our ancestors—their struggles and their triumphs. These stories imbued the dish with an emotional depth, making every bite a connection to our roots.

During Onam, our family would come together for the traditional sadya feast, and Ammumma's Puli Inji would take the centre stage. The first bite always transported us to a world filled with memories and the warmth of togetherness.

Puli Inji represents the harmony of sweet and sour, much like the balance of life itself. It reminds us that even amid chaos, there is beauty in balance.

PULI INJI
(Tamarind Ginger Relish)

BINU MENON — KERALA

SERVES: 10 — PREPARATION TIME: 15 MINUTES

COOK TIME: 30 MINUTES

INGREDIENTS

Tamarind	70 gms
Jaggery	120 gms
Turmeric powder	½ tsp
Chilli powder	1½ tsp
Asafoetida	¼ tsp
Salt	to taste
Water	250 ml
Coconut oil	4 tbsp
Mustard seeds	1 tsp
Urad dal (split and dehusked black gram)	1 tsp
Curry leaves	10
Dry red chillies	2, finely chopped
Ginger	100 gms, peeled and finely chopped
Green chillies	4, finely chopped

METHOD

Soak the tamarind in 250 ml of hot water for 10 minutes. Squeeze the tamarind to extract the pulp and strain it to remove any residue.

Transfer the tamarind pulp water into an earthen pot or kadhai.

Add jaggery, turmeric powder, chilli powder, asafoetida, and salt to the tamarind water. Bring the mixture to a boil and let it simmer till it thickens.

In a separate pan, heat coconut oil and add mustard seeds. Let them splutter.

Add urad dal, dry red chillies, and curry leaves to it. Sauté for about a minute.

Add the chopped ginger and green chillies to the pan. Fry till the ginger turns golden brown.

Pour this tempering or tadka to the tamarind-jaggery mixture. Simmer for another 5 minutes to combine the flavours.

Once cooled, store it in a glass container. Serve fresh or refrigerate it for later use.

Serving suggestion: Serve as a pickle/chutney.

Vankaya Tomato Pachadi by Sumalya Guttikonda, Andhra Pradesh

I feel incredibly proud to share this Vankaya Tomato Pachadi recipe from my hometown in Andhra Pradesh. I learned this cherished recipe from my mother, who is renowned in our family for her chutneys. Whenever relatives, especially my aunts, visit, they eagerly request her delicious creations. These chutneys have become a highlight of our family gatherings, showcasing her exceptional culinary skills, infused with love and affection.

Now, this cherished chutney is a staple in my home, and I am determined to pass on this legacy to my children. They are excited to savour and share these priceless family recipes in the future, as they, too, are ardent admirers of their nani's chutneys.

VANKAYA TOMATO PACHADI
(Spicy Tangy Tomato–Brinjal Chutney)

SUMALYA GUTTIKONDA — ANDHRA PRADESH

SERVES: 5 — PREPARATION TIME: 15 MINUTES

COOK TIME: 30 MINUTES

INGREDIENTS

Brinjals	250 gms
Tomatoes	2, medium-sized

Oil	1 tsp
Green chillies	6–8, slit longitudinally
Tamarind	7–10 gms, deseeded and to taste
Cumin seeds	1 tsp
Garlic	6 cloves
Onion	1, medium-sized, finely chopped, to garnish
Salt	to taste

METHOD

Chop the brinjals and tomatoes into medium-sized cubes.

Heat 1 tsp of oil in a wok over medium heat.

Add the chopped brinjals and green chillies. Sprinkle salt and sauté them until they soften.

Add the chopped tomatoes to the wok and continue frying them.

Allow the mixture to cool completely.

Transfer the cooled mixture to a blender. Add cumin seeds, garlic, and tamarind, and then blend into a coarse paste.

Garnish with finely chopped onions before serving.

Serving suggestion: Serve it with steamed rice and ghee for the best taste!

Gajar Gobhi Achaar
by Purnima Rao, Punjab

Gajar Gobhi Achaar holds a special place in my heart, as it is my grandfather's recipe, cherished by our family, especially during winters. When we were kids, my grandfather would prepare this pickle in a large wok and distribute it to all his daughters and grandchildren. I can still recall his smile and the love he poured into making it.

Every winter, I eagerly look forward to making this pickle myself, as its rich blend of spices adds such incredible flavours that it can elevate even a plain chapati into something special.

GAJAR GOBHI ACHAAR
(Carrot and Cauliflower Pickle)

PURNIMA RAO — PUNJAB

MAKES: 5 KGS (APPROX.) — PREPARATION TIME: 3 DAYS

COOK TIME: 30 MINUTES

INGREDIENTS

Carrots	2.5 kgs
Cauliflowers	2.5 kgs
Onions	1 kg, sliced
Ginger	150 gms
Garlic	150 gms

Mustard oil	1 ltr
Cinnamon	50 gms
Black cardamom	100 gms
Cumin seeds	100 gms, roasted
Mace	20 gms
Nutmeg	2 pieces
Mustard seeds	50 gms
Red chilli powder	5 tbsp
Turmeric powder	10 tbsp
Salt	10 tbsp
Sugar	500 gms
Black vinegar	350 ml

METHOD

Wash the carrots and cauliflowers thoroughly. Cut them into small pieces and dry them in sunlight for 2 days.

After 2 days, heat mustard oil in a pan and fry the sun-dried vegetables. Set them aside.

Heat mustard oil in a pan again and fry the sliced onions. Set them aside.

Make a paste of garlic and ginger, add it to the fried onions, and cook for 2–3 minutes until browned. Ensure no water is added at any step.

Then, take cinnamon, black cardamom, roasted cumin seeds, mace, nutmeg, and mustard seeds, and grind them all into a coarse powder.

Add the coarsely ground spices, red chilli powder, turmeric powder, salt, and sugar into the black vinegar. Boil it for some time to allow the sugar to dissolve properly. Take it off the flame and add it to the onion-ginger-garlic mixture.

Add the fried carrots and cauliflowers to this prepared masala. Mix well to ensure the vegetables are evenly coated with the spices.

Transfer the pickle into a clean and dry glass jar. Let it sit overnight to develop its flavours.

Your Gajar Gobhi Achaar is now ready to enjoy!

Sweets

Bhapa Doi

by Neha Srivastava, West Bengal

Our family hails from a rich tapestry of cultures and regions, with a passion for food that unites us all. As a Defence family, our lives have been enriched with traditions from across the country. Among the many cuisines we cherish, Bengali food holds a special place in our hearts. This love isn't just limited to our immediate family; it resonates throughout our extended clan as well. The credit for introducing this beloved Bengali delicacy, Bhapa Doi, to our family goes largely to my father. During his posting at Barrackpore in Kolkata—the oldest cantonment in India—Dad came across this exquisite dessert at a quaint sweet shop while running a routine errand.

Captivated by its unique taste, he was determined to recreate it at home. With his keen interest in cooking, he sought out the head cook of the Officer's Mess to learn the base recipe and its various adaptations. After a few experimental trials in our kitchen, Dad perfected his version of Bhapa Doi, turning it into his signature dish.

Now, at 70 years old, he continues to relish making this dessert, often involving his grandkids in the process. This recipe is a cherished family heirloom.

BHAPA DOI
(Steamed Yogurt)

NEHA SRIVASTAVA | WEST BENGAL

SERVES: 10 | PREPARATION TIME: 10 MINUTES

COOK TIME: 20 MINUTES

INGREDIENTS

Hung curd	500 gms
Sugar	100 gms, powdered, or to taste
Cardamom powder	1 tsp
Saffron	12 strands
Almonds	1 tsp, slivered
Pistachio	1 tsp, slivered
Dried rose petals (optional)	1 tsp
Chironji (cuddapah almonds) (optional)	½ tsp, chopped
Lukewarm milk	2 tsp

METHOD

Soak six saffron strands in lukewarm milk and set aside.

In a bowl, mix hung curd, sugar, cardamom powder, and the prepared saffron milk. Stir until smooth and well combined.

Pour this mixture evenly into small pudding bowls or ramekins.

Sprinkle chopped dry fruits, rose petals, and the remaining saffron strands on top.

Place the ramekins in a steamer and cook on medium heat for 20 minutes until the mixture sets.

Remove the ramekins from the steamer, allow them to cool slightly, and refrigerate for at least 30 minutes to cool and set.

Bhapa Doi is ready to be served!

Note: To prepare hung curd, place regular curd in a muslin cloth or fine sieve and let it drain for at least 2 hours to remove excess water. For best results, leave it overnight in the refrigerator. One kilogram of regular curd typically yields about 500 grams of thick, creamy hung curd, which is ideal for this recipe. It's essential to use curd made from full-fat milk, as skimmed or low-fat options won't provide the desired richness and texture.

When sweetening the mixture, adjust the sugar according to your preference and taste the blend before pouring it into the bowls. For a mildly sweet Bhapa Doi, 100 grams of sugar is often sufficient. Use small ramekins or porcelain bowls for steaming, as they distribute heat evenly and ensure the dessert sets beautifully. If you don't have a dedicated steamer, a momo or idli steamer works just as well, or you can improvise with a large steel pot and a tight-fitting lid.

Dudhi Kulfi

by Radhika Bakshi, New Delhi

This kulfi recipe comes from my maternal grandma and was often made by my mother. It boasts a luscious, creamy texture and the subtle flavour of elaichi (cardamom), complemented by the deep caramel undertones of full-cream milk and sugar, slow-cooked for hours to achieve that thick, creamy, rabri-like consistency and taste with a brownish tint. What makes it truly special is the addition of the goodness of humble lauki! My dad loved having this kulfi with roohafza while my mum always made a chocolate-flavoured batch for us kids.

For me, this kulfi is more than just a dessert; it's a piece of my mum's unconditional love and joy in cooking for her family. I can feel it every time I make it. She left us 14 years ago to reunite with my dad, but the taste of her cooking remains permanently etched in my heart and soul. I'm sharing this Dudhi Kulfi recipe that my mum, the late Mrs Neelam Arora, used to make.

DUDHI KULFI
(Bottle Gourd Kulfi)

RADHIKA BAKSHI | NEW DELHI

SERVES: 4–6 | PREPARATION TIME: 1.5–2 HOURS

COOK TIME: 8 HOURS OR OVERNIGHT IN FREEZER

INGREDIENTS

Bottle gourd	300–400 gms, medium-sized, grated
Full cream milk	2 ltrs
Sugar	80 gms or to taste
Cardamom powder	1 tsp
Saffron (optional)	15–20 strands, soaked in 2 tbsp warm milk

METHOD

In a large, thick-bottomed wok, bring the milk to a full boil.

Meanwhile, pressure cook the grated bottle gourd without any water for two whistles.

Add the boiled bottle gourd to the boiling milk. Simmer on medium to low flame, stirring occasionally to prevent burning, until the milk reduces to almost half and the bottle gourd becomes completely mushy.

Once the milk has reduced, add the sugar and cardamom powder. Continue cooking until the mixture thickens to a rabri-like consistency or the texture of a thick custard.

After approximately 1.5 hours of slow cooking, the kulfi mixture will have a light pink hue, the hallmark of a well-cooked rabri.

Now, add saffron to the mixture and cook for an additional 1–2 minutes. Switch off the gas and allow it to cool completely.

Then, transfer this mixture to a blender. Blend it into a smooth batter.

Transfer the blended mixture into a container of your choice. Cover it with a cling film pressed lightly onto the surface to prevent icicle formation, then freeze for at least 5–6 hours or overnight.

Before serving, let the kulfi sit at room temperature for a couple of minutes to soften slightly.

Serving suggestion: Serve chilled with a splash of roohafza or rose syrup, falooda, and soaked basil seeds. Alternatively, savour this frozen delight in its pure, creamy form!

Gulgula

by Rachna Shukla, Uttar Pradesh

Gulgula—the name alone takes me back to my childhood, evoking memories of warmth, celebration, and family. My mother and grandmothers would make this dish for every special occasion, whether it was Diwali, Karwa Chauth, or my birthday.

Yes, it was even a birthday special! Unlike today, my birthday was celebrated with a puja at home. After the Dev Puja, Mumma would lovingly put a tilak on my forehead, drape a garland around my neck, and then offer me a glass of milk with freshly-made Gulgule. Ah! Those beautiful moments are unforgettable. To me, Gulgula is synonymous with my childhood.

Ironically, I never liked Gulgula as a child, though I couldn't quite pinpoint why. Yet today, as I prepare it for special occasions, I find myself relishing not just the taste, but the memories and traditions it represents. It's funny how something I once dismissed has now become something I deeply treasure.

GULGULA
(Sweet Wheat Flour Dumplings)

RACHNA SHUKLA — UTTAR PRADESH

SERVES: 4 — PREPARATION TIME: 15 MINUTES

COOK TIME:15 MINUTES

INGREDIENTS

Whole wheat flour	65 gms
Sugar	80 gms
Fennel seeds	½ tsp
Black pepper powder	1 pinch
Nutmeg powder	1 pinch
Desi ghee	200 gms, melted
Water	4–5 tbsp (approx.)

METHOD

In a dry bowl, mix whole wheat flour, sugar, fennel seeds, black pepper powder, nutmeg powder, and 1 teaspoon of desi ghee.

Gradually add water in small batches to make a thick batter. Test the consistency by scooping the batter with a spoon and inverting it; if the batter takes a little time to fall, it's perfect.

Now, beat the batter vigorously for about 10 minutes until it becomes fluffy.

Heat the rest of the ghee in a wok over medium-high heat.

To check if the ghee is ready, put one drop of batter in it. If the batter rises to the surface immediately without changing colour, the ghee is at the correct temperature.

Using a teaspoon, slowly drop small portions of batter (the size of a teaspoon approximately) into the heated ghee. Avoid overcrowding the wok and fry 4–5 gulgulas at a time. Cook until they turn golden brown on all sides, turning them occasionally. Each batch should take 2 to 3 minutes.

Remove the fried gulgulas and place them on a paper towel to absorb excess ghee.

Serve hot or even when cooled; they taste yummy either way!

Note: When preparing the gulgula batter, it's important to check the consistency, as a batter that is too thick will result in chewy gulgulas, while one that is too thin will make them overly crispy. To test if the batter is ready for frying, take a small portion and drop it into a glass of water. If it sinks, continue beating the batter for a bit longer to incorporate more air. However, if it floats, the batter is ready to be fried. Additionally, ensure that the ghee is sufficiently hot before frying; if it's not hot enough, the gulgulas will sink to the bottom of the wok instead of floating and cooking evenly. Fry 4–5 gulgulas at a time, turning them occasionally, until they are golden brown on all sides, and be mindful not to overcrowd the wok as that would result in uneven cooking.

Haldi ki Pinni

by Deepa Verma, Punjab

In the heart of Punjab, in a quaint village named Lohia, my dadi, a striking 5-feet-7-inches tall woman with an exceptional talent for both cooking and crocheting, created dishes that were nothing short of magical. Her kitchen was a sanctuary of heavenly flavours, where even a simple Mathra Pulao became a feast fit for royalty.

Among her many culinary gems, one recipe stands out—Haldi ki Pinni. This dish is a testament to Dadi's culinary genius. Known for its health benefits, particularly in healing internal injuries and boosting overall wellness, these pinnis blend taste and nutrition perfectly.

Today, this recipe is a highlight at our family gatherings and a weekend favourite at home. Every time I prepare Haldi ki Pinni, it feels as if Dadi is right there with me, guiding my hands and filling the house with the warmth of her love. It's not just food; it's a piece of my heritage, a slice of nostalgia, and a bowl full of love.

Making Haldi ki Pinni is more than just following a recipe; it's about honouring Dadi's legacy and sharing a piece of our history with every bite. This dish binds us together, generation after generation, reminding us of the simple joys and rich traditions that make our family unique.

So, here's to Dadi and her incredible Haldi ki Pinni—a dish

made with love, from our kitchen to yours. Enjoy these pinnis with a glass of milk for a perfect start to your day, and remember to store them in the fridge to keep their freshness and benefits intact.

HALDI KI PINNI
(Turmeric Energy Balls)

DEEPA VERMA — PUNJAB

MAKES: 1 KG — PREPARATION TIME: 15 MINUTES

COOK TIME: 40 MINUTES

INGREDIENTS

Raw turmeric	250 gms, washed, peeled, and grated
Desi ghee	500 gms
Milk	1 ltr
Besan (chickpea flour)	250 gms
Almonds	100 gms, chopped
Cashews	100 gms, chopped
Raisins	50 gms
Jaggery/Desi khaand	500 gms, grated

METHOD

Start by thoroughly washing the raw turmeric. Peel and grate it. (It would be helpful to wear gloves for this step as raw turmeric will stain your hands yellow.)

In a pan, heat 250 grams of ghee. Add the grated raw turmeric and cook it over a low flame for about 10 minutes, stirring occasionally.

Once the turmeric is sautéed, pour in 1 litre of milk. Keep stirring until all the milk vaporizes and the mixture thickens.

In a separate pan, heat the remaining 250 grams of ghee and add besan. Roast it over medium heat, stirring continuously, until it turns golden brown.

Combine the cooked turmeric mix and the roasted besan in one pan. Stir well to evenly blend everything together.

Add the chopped dry fruits to the pan. Mix well and roast for another 5 minutes.

Add the grated jaggery to the mixture. Stir continuously until the jaggery melts and blends in completely.

Remove the pan from the stove and let it cool slightly. While it's still warm, shape the mixture into small balls (pinnis). Let the pinnis cool completely and then store them in an airtight container.

Enjoy your nutritious and delicious Haldi ki Pinni!

Note: You can adjust the amount of jaggery/desi khaand and dry fruits according to your taste.

Storage: To maintain freshness, store these Haldi ki Pinnis in the fridge. Due to the milk content, they can spoil quickly if left out at room temperature. Keep them chilled to enjoy their benefits for longer. Simply heat a little before eating.

Hayagreeva
by Deepa Kulkarni, Karnataka

My ajji would make this dish during festivals, a beloved tradition in our Madhwa community. This prasada is lovingly prepared at Vadirajaru Matha in Sonda. Ajji made it even more special by reciting shlokas while preparing it in madi—a sacred practice where food is cooked in a special way, on a wood fire, while wearing damp clothes and keeping the mind free from negative thoughts.

For Madhwas, cooking is not merely an art; it's a form of service to God and a deeply spiritual experience. Preparing this dish allows me to connect my present to my past, keeping my heritage alive.

HAYAGREEVA
(Sweet Chana Dal Dessert with Jaggery and Nuts)

DEEPA KULKARNI — KARNATAKA

SERVES: 4 — PREPARATION TIME: 30 MINUTES

COOK TIME: 30 MINUTES

INGREDIENTS

Chana dal	100 gms
Turmeric powder	a pinch
Ghee	½ tsp

Water	200 ml (approx.)
Jaggery	75 gms, powdered
Poppy seeds	1.5 tbsp, dry roasted
Desiccated coconut	2 tbsp

FOR GARNISHING:

Ghee	3–4 tbsp
Cashews	8–10
Raisins	8–10

METHOD

Soak the chana dal in water for about 30 minutes.

Pressure cook the soaked chana dal with a pinch of turmeric and half a teaspoon of ghee for three whistles. The chana dal should become soft while maintaining its shape. Soaking it before cooking ensures it cooks well.

Once the pressure releases, add jaggery and cook till it melts and the mixture thickens slightly.

When it starts to thicken, add the roasted poppy seeds and grated coconut. Cook for a couple of minutes, then turn off the stove.

For the garnish, heat ghee in a separate pan, add the cashews, and fry till they turn brown. Add the raisins and turn off the flame immediately.

Pour this over the chana dal jaggery mix and stir well.

Your Hayagreeva is ready to be savoured!

Note: Make sure to set aside some time for a Hayagreeva–induced nap after this delightful treat!

Kesariya Gulab Kheer
by Mukti Agarwal, Uttar Pradesh

My bauji (maternal grandfather) had a serious sweet tooth, and so does my father. Not surprisingly, this love for sweets was passed down to my sister and me as well. During our vacations at nanihaal, it was a task for Ammaji (my maternal grandmother) to ensure we had our fill of as many sweets as she could prepare. Despite always making a plethora of stuff for us to gorge on, my favourite memory is walking into her home and being greeted by the most beautiful aroma of the saffron-induced sweetness with hints of cardamom and rose. My first meal at Nani's house was inevitably the absolutely mouth-watering, delicious kesariya gulab rice kheer she made, paired with Ajwain ki Poori! It may sound like a weird combination for some, but for me, it is still the best dish that reminds me of 'Nani ke haath ka pyaar (Nani's love)'.

KESARIYA GULAB KHEER
(Saffron Rose Rice Pudding)

MUKTI AGARWAL | UTTAR PRADESH

SERVES: 6 | PREPARATION TIME: 15 MINUTES

COOK TIME: 2 HOURS 30 MINUTES

INGREDIENTS

Basmati rice	65 gms
Desi ghee	5 tsp
Full fat milk	1 ltr
Water	50 ml
Sugar	6–8 tbsp
Saffron	15–20 strands
Green cardamom	5–6, powdered
Almonds	20, roasted and chopped
Cashews	20, roasted and chopped
Raisins (optional)	20
Dried rose petals	to garnish

METHOD

Rinse the rice well until the water runs clear. Soak it in fresh water for 2–4 hours, or until the grains can easily be broken with your fingers. Drain the water completely.

Heat 5 teaspoons of desi ghee in a pan, then add the drained rice and cook it in the ghee for 5–10 minutes. Keep the rice aside.

Take a heavy-bottomed pan and add 50 ml of water (this helps prevent the kheer from getting scorched).

Add the milk and bring it to a boil, stirring frequently to avoid the milk sticking to the bottom of the pan.

Lower the flame and add the drained rice to the milk. Cook for another 55–60 minutes, stirring frequently, until the rice is fully cooked and the milk starts to thicken.

Add sugar and stir to combine. Continue cooking for another 45 minutes and the kheer reaches a thick consistency.

Add the saffron strands and mix well. You will instantly see your kheer turning a beautiful shade of yellow. Keep stirring continuously to prevent burning.

Stir in the powdered cardamom, raisins, almonds, and cashews, and cook until the kheer reaches your desired consistency.

Let it cool and then refrigerate for a few hours.

Garnish it with chopped nuts and dried rose petals before serving.

Serving suggestion: Kesariya Gulab Kheer is best served chilled and pairs well with Ajwain wali Poori.

Puran Poli

by Seema Jain Krishnan, Maharashtra

Puran Poli is a sweet and aromatic Indian flatbread that symbolizes celebration, tradition, and a good harvest in Maharashtra. This delightful treat is a staple during festivals such as Gudhi Padwa, Akshaya Tritiya, Ganesh Chaturthi, and Holi.

My mother, a proud Maharashtrian, has always cherished Puran Poli, and it has become one of my all-time favourites as well. I was fortunate enough to learn this authentic recipe from her, and it brings me great joy to have consistently received her compliments for making it just like she does.

The traditional filling for these puran polis has a mixture of split Bengal gram (chana dal), jaggery, cardamom, and nutmeg. Some families also add grated coconut for an extra layer of richness, though it's optional. The jaggery imparts a healthy sweetness, while the cardamom and nutmeg lend a rich, fragrant, and slightly spicy flavour.

The process involves stuffing the puran inside the prepared dough, rolling it into thin flatbreads, and cooking them on a hot griddle with a generous amount of ghee until both sides develop a beautiful golden-brown colour. Puran Poli is best enjoyed warm, with an extra dollop of ghee on top.

I'm excited to share this authentic Puran Poli recipe, adding a touch of tradition and flavour to your festive celebrations. Happy cooking!

PURAN POLI
(Sweet Lentil-stuffed Flatbread)

SEEMA JAIN KRISHNAN | MAHARASHTRA

MAKES: 6–8 MEDIUM–SIZED POLIS | PREPARATION TIME: 90 MINUTES

COOK TIME: 30 MINUTES

INGREDIENTS

FOR THE PURAN (SWEET LENTIL FILLING):

Chana dal	200 gms
Water	240 ml (for cooking dal)
Desi ghee	2 tbsp
Green cardamom	½ tsp, powdered
Nutmeg powder	¼ tsp
Jaggery or jaggery powder	200 gms (grated, if using jaggery)
Sugar	50 gms

FOR THE POLI (OUTER COVERING):

Whole wheat flour	175 gms
Maida (all-purpose flour)	60 gms
Desi ghee	4 tbsp
Salt	¼ tsp
Turmeric powder (optional)	¼ teaspoon
Water	300 ml (approx., for kneading the dough)
Desi ghee	100 gms or as required

METHOD

For preparing puran (sweet lentil filling)

Rinse the chana dal thoroughly in water and soak it overnight (or at least for an hour if in a rush). Drain the water.

In a pressure cooker, cook the chana dal with 240 ml of

water for 6 to 7 whistles, ensuring the dal is cooked well and becomes mushy.

Once cooked, strain the cooked dal using a sieve, making sure to remove all excess water. (Keep the stock aside. It can be added to your everyday cooking for roti or vegetables.)

Heat 2 tbsp ghee in a pan and add the ground nutmeg and ground cardamom. Fry these spices for a few seconds on low heat.

Add the cooked chana dal, jaggery, and sugar. Stir well and let this mixture cook on low heat till the mixture becomes dry. Stir frequently to avoid burning.

Allow it to cool and make large balls from the mixture for the filling.

For preparing the poli dough

Combine all the poli ingredients and kneed them into a smooth, pliable dough.

For making Puran Poli

Take a medium-sized ball of dough and roll it out to about 2 to 3 inches in circumference on a dusted rolling board.

Place a portion of the prepared puran mixture in the centre of the rolled dough. Bring the edges together towards the centre, then pinch them to seal.

Sprinkle some flour on the dough and gently roll it out to form a medium or large circle, depending on the amount of dough and puran filling used.

Heat a tawa or griddle and spread some ghee. Place the rolled Puran Poli on the tawa. When one side turns light brown, flip it over and cook the other side till you see some brownish spots.

Once both sides are browned, turn the Puran Poli over,

apply some ghee, and cook it until both sides have golden-brown spots.

Repeat this process for the remaining Puran Polis and stack them in a casserole.

Serving suggestion: Puran Poli can be served warm or at room temperature with milk, ghee, or yogurt. However, it is best enjoyed warm with an extra dollop of ghee on it.

Sarkkarai Pongal

by Subhashini Ramasubramanian, Tamil Nadu

Sarkkarai Pongal is a dish deeply tied to our heritage, especially during the harvest festival of Pongal, when freshly harvested rice and dal are used to make this beloved dish. It's one of our family favourites, often associated with family gatherings, festivals, and special occasions. The memories of preparing and eating this dish together only add to its appeal, making it a favourite not just for its taste but for the cherished moments it represents.

Made with simple ingredients like rice, lentils, jaggery, and ghee, Sarkkarai Pongal is a traditional sweet dish prepared in South Indian households and temples for special occasions and offered to the Gods. The softness of the rice cooked in milk, the sweetness of jaggery, and the richness of ghee come together in every bite. The nuts and raisins add a delightful texture, making it both comforting and indulgent. It's a connection to our roots and culture, a reminder of our Tamil festivals. It's special because it brings everyone back home, reminding us of family and togetherness!

SARKKARAI PONGAL
(Sweet Rice Pudding)

SUBHASHINI RAMASUBRAMANIAN — TAMIL NADU

SERVES: 3–4 — PREPARATION TIME: 20 MINUTES

COOK TIME: 2 HOURS 20 MINUTES

INGREDIENTS

Rice	200 gms (any South Indian rice variety)
Split yellow moong dal	50 gms
Jaggery	300 gms or to taste, grated
Milk	250 ml
Desi ghee	50 ml, melted
Cardamom powder	1 pinch
Cashews	10–15, roasted in ghee
Raisins	10–15, roasted in ghee

METHOD

The dal and rice can be cooked together. This can either be done in a pressure cooker or in a heavy-bottomed vessel. Both methods are shared here.

For both the methods, you can dry roast the rice and dal slightly before cooking them as this results in a more flavourful and aromatic dish. However, this step is optional.

In a pressure cooker

For 200 grams rice and 50 grams dal, add 250 ml of milk and 850 ml of water in a pressure cooker. Mix well and close the lid. Cook for about 5–6 whistles.

Switch off the gas and let the cooker cool down naturally and release the pressure leftover before opening.

Remove the lid and check the consistency of the rice and dal mixture. It has to be very soft and mushy. Mash it well using a big ladle and keep it aside.

In a heavy-bottomed vessel

In a vessel, add a mixture of 250 ml of milk and 850 ml of water. Bring it to a boil.

When the milk starts to boil and is about to overflow, add the rice and dal mixture. Cook till the mixture is soft and mushy, adding more water or milk.

This method takes longer than a pressure cooker.

Once the rice and dal are cooked in any one of the above methods, in a heavy-bottomed kadhai, add 2 tablespoons of ghee. Then, add the cooked dal and rice mixture. If you used a heavy-bottomed vessel for cooking, continue using the same vessel.

Keep the flame low and add the grated jaggery. Stir occasionally as the jaggery melts. Continue mixing until the mixture becomes runny but doesn't stick to the bottom. If needed, add more ghee.

Let the mixture cook until it starts to thicken and small bubbles form. Adjust the flame to low to prevent it from sticking.

Once the mixture has thickened, and the aroma of jaggery and ghee fills the air, check the consistency. Do not let it become too thick and sticky.

When ready, turn off the flame. Transfer the Pongal to a serving dish to prevent further thickening from the residual heat.

Now, add green cardamom, roasted cashews, roasted raisins, and the remaining ghee.

As the preparation cools down, it will thicken a bit more.

Sarkkarai Pongal is ready to serve!

Serving suggestion: This dish is best served warm. It can also be topped with a teaspoon of melted ghee and a few roasted cashews and raisins for extra richness.

Note: The amount of jaggery can be adjusted as per preference.

Thekua

by Anshu Singh, Bihar / Uttar Pradesh

Thekua is a dry, sweet snack from Bihar and Uttar Pradesh, made with simple ingredients like wheat flour, jaggery or sugar, and ghee. For a hardcore Bihari like me, Thekua is a blend of emotions that brings a sparkle to my eyes, a smile to my lips, and countless memories to my mind. It is the main prasad of the world-famous Chhath Puja.

My grandmother, a brave freedom fighter and a principal of a government school, prepared Thekua with utmost dedication and love. As teenagers, we would assist her in its preparation during Chhath Puja, and that is why Thekua holds such a special place in my heart.

THEKUA
(Fried Wheat Flour and Jaggery Cookies)

ANSHU SINGH — BIHAR/UTTAR PRADESH

SERVES: 20 — PREPARATION TIME: 30 MINUTES

COOK TIME: 30 MINUTES

INGREDIENTS

Wheat flour	1.25 kg
Jaggery	400 gms

Desi ghee (preferably, cow ghee)	1.5 kg
Fennel seeds	2 tsp
Dry coconut	50 gms
Cardamom powder	1 tsp
Water	200 ml (approx.)

METHOD

Take jaggery in a bowl and break it into small pieces. Add one cup of warm water and stir until the jaggery dissolves completely.

Then, in a paraat, combine wheat flour and 200 grams of melted warm desi ghee. Mix it properly and mash it with your hands for 10 minutes, ensuring it's thoroughly blended.

Add fennel seeds, dry coconut, and cardamom powder to the wheat flour mixture, and mix again. Gradually pour in the jaggery water, mixing it well with both hands after each addition. The dough should come together and have a smooth, pliable texture.

Shape the dough into small balls. Put these balls, one at a time, on a wooden saancha (a special wooden platform used to make Thekua) and gently press down to flatten.

Meanwhile, heat ghee in a kadhai over medium-low heat. Once the ghee is hot, carefully add the shaped thekuas and deep fry them until they turn light brown, ensuring even frying on both sides. Once golden brown, remove the thekuas from the ghee, and drain them on paper towels.

Thekua is ready to serve.

Serving suggestion: Thekua can be enjoyed either hot or cold.

Note: They can also be stored in an airtight container to maintain their freshness and extending their shelf life.

Ingredient Index

Fruits

Glueberry

Jaggery

Kokum

Lemon

Lentils

Milk

Mutton

Acknowledgements

A project as special as *Flavours of India: Heirloom Recipes from India's Kitchens* is only possible because of the passion, dedication, and hard work of an incredible team.

A heartfelt thank you to:

Sobana Laxmi Kevin, whose meticulous management and curation ensured that every recipe found its rightful place in this collection.

Mukti Agarwal, for her keen editorial eye and attention to detail in refining each recipe, making them clear and easy to follow.

Ambika Rikhye, for beautifully weaving storytelling into the book, bringing the heart and history of each dish to life.

Anshu Bhatia, for seamlessly coordinating with our contributors, ensuring we had the perfect recipes and pictures to showcase the essence of Indian kitchens.

To the entire GurgaonMoms community—thank you for sharing your treasured recipes, stories, and culinary traditions. This book is a celebration of your love for food and the vibrant flavours that define India's kitchens.

Finally, to every reader and home cook—may these heirloom recipes bring warmth to your kitchen and joy to your table for generations to come.